I0035382

The Management Map...
Navigation Tools for the New Manager

Deborah Avrin, MS, SPHR

ManageSmart Publishing

This publication contains the opinions and ideas of the author. The author and publisher specifically disclaim all responsibility for any liability, loss, or risk, personal or otherwise, that is incurred as a consequence, directly or indirectly, of the uses and applications of this book. Any and all implied or expressed warranties of fitness are hereby disclaimed.

Copyright 2008, Deborah Avrin
All rights reserved. No part of this book may be reproduced, stored in a retrieval system, or transmitted by any means, electronic, mechanical, photocopying, recording, or otherwise, without written permission from the author.

Published by ManageSmart Publishing
Plano, Texas
972-881-5282

Printed in the United States of America

ISBN: 978-0-9820901-0-7
Cover design: MC2 Graphics

To my parents, Ruth and John Happ, for always believing in me.

CONTENTS

ACKNOWLEDGMENTS

They say "you get by with a little help from your friends." The support I've received from my friends and family in making *The Management Map* a reality has been overwhelming. Without their help, this book would never have gone from the thoughts and ideas I had in my head to written words on the page.

Thank you to Erica Avrin, Sara Belmontes, Fiona Hunter, Shari Kenerson, Danielle McNett, John Mooney, and Lisa Smith for taking the time out of your busy lives to read manuscript drafts and provide feedback. John and Fiona did a great job on a rough first draft and they "volunteered" to review a second draft, going above and beyond in offering valuable feedback. Sara provided up-to-date technology information. Erica and Shari consistently reminded me that "commas are our friends."

This project has afforded me the opportunity to work with a terrific group of professionals, including my book coach and friend Sharon Redd, who provided step-by-step advice and inspiration; cover designer Alan McCuller; editor Martha McCuller; and my accountant, Gene Sumerall, who pestered me to write this book. Yes Gene, I finally finished the book!

Finally I would like to thank my husband, Stuart, for joining me on life's journey

INTRODUCTION

Congratulations! You have achieved your goal of becoming a manager. You are very excited about the opportunity, but probably have concerns, too. You might be thinking:

"What does a manager actually DO?"
"What does my boss expect?"
"How will I be successful?"
"I've got PEOPLE! Now what?"

Moving from an individual contributor to a manager is one of the biggest leaps someone can make in his or her career.

I like to think of management as a journey. If you were traveling to a new place what would you do: purchase a map or travel guide?

Wouldn't it be great if you had such a map for your management journey? A map that contained practical tips for the new manager. A map to shorten the learning curve and increase your confidence that you will be successful.

The Management Map: Navigation Tools for the New Manager is just such a travel planner. It provides answers to common questions such as:
- Which way will I go?
- Who will I take with me?
- How will I measure progress?
- When will I go?
- How will I handle roadblocks, detours, and speed bumps along the way?
- When will I need to stop and get or give directions?

Each chapter contains a wealth of practical tips that I have learned during a career in human resources, and in developing and delivering management programs to a wide client base. These tips will get your management journey started in the right direction. At the end of each chapter is a list of follow-up activities and training topics to help you continue to build your own management map.

Enjoy the journey!

ONE

VISUALIZING YOUR MANAGEMENT MAP... How Will You Go?

Chapter Learning Points:
- Create your management vision
- Identify your managerial competencies

> *"To begin with the end in mind means to start with a clear understanding of your destination. It means to know where you're going so that you better understand where you are now and so that the steps you take are always in the right direction."*
>
> ~Stephen R. Covey, author, *The 7 Habits of Highly Effective People*

Congratulations on Your Retirement!

Whoa! Why are we talking about retirement in a book for new managers? Just as you read a map from your point of departure to your destination, the beginning of your management journey is the best place to think about the end of your journey. Every step along the way, every action you take during your journey, will

1

ultimately impact the manager you eventually will become. Here is a story to illustrate:

John reflects on his journey as a manager and his impact on others. He has decided to retire after a long and satisfying career and his organization is rewarding him with a retirement party. They have asked his long-time colleague and friend Ed to locate as many people as possible who have worked with John over the years. Even though Ed is the kind of guy who enjoys keeping track of former colleagues, John can't believe the number of people that Ed has located. These individuals are not only able to attend the party, but are also willing to speak about what their association with John has meant to them

The big day comes and John is a little apprehensive about what he will hear. Ten of John's former employees and managers are on the agenda to speak. Ed told John that he had to turn away many more people who wanted to speak.

One by one, John's former employees come to the podium and speak about the difference John has made in their lives. They include a sprinkling of good-natured jokes, of course.

"John was the type of manager who made me believe I could succeed at anything."

"If it wasn't for John's mentoring, I never would have applied for, and received, my first promotion."

"When I received my first managerial position, I remembered John's management style and used that as my role model."

Then it was time for a few of John's former managers to speak about what it was like to have him on their teams.

"I always could count on John to manage with integrity. The employees on his team were committed and achieved great results for the company."

"John had a great way of getting his employees excited about work. He was a role model for other managers and made my job much easier."

In addition to the testimonials, John accumulated a large stack of notes and cards from well-wishers. "I had no idea that I had such an impact on people's lives!" John expressed in amazement.

Now, flash forward to the end of your career as a manager. If this were your retirement party, what would your former employees and managers comment about you? What comments would you like to hear?

Creating Your Management Vision

As you begin your journey, you are in a unique position to visualize the type of manager you want to become. The management vision you create provides the direction to guide your course and the choices you make about your career. This vision acts as a series of lampposts that light the path of your journey. You move closer and closer to your vision by developing skills and competencies until you are proficient, and the vision then becomes a reality.

> *Your vision is the promise of what you shall one day be. One who cherishes a beautiful vision, a lofty ideal, will one day realize it.*
>
> ~James Allen, author, *As a Man Thinketh*

How will you create your vision? Here are a few questions to think about and answer:

- What two to three things must be present in your environment for you to feel fulfilled in your work?

- What are five to six of your most important values? (Examples include: integrity, competence, variety, freedom, prosperity, benevolence, cooperation, etc.)

- When your management career is ending, what will you regret not doing, seeing, or achieving?

- What strengths do you see in yourself? What have others said about your strengths?

After you have thought about and written your answers to the previous questions, you can start to visualize the future. It may sound a bit unusual, but for this part it is helpful to close your eyes. Picture yourself performing the duties of a manager and consider such things as:

- What does your environment look like?

- What are you doing and saying?
- What are other people doing and saying?
- What successes are you celebrating?
- What are your facial expressions and body language as you interact with your team members?
- How do other people describe you?

You are now ready to write a managerial vision statement. It is best to write in the first person and make statements about the future you hope to achieve. Write the statements as if you are already making them happen in your life. Some experts recommend 50 words or less.

Committing your management vision to paper helps encourage your commitment to its accomplishment. If you want to take this activity one step further, you can create a "vision board," also known as a goal map, dream board, or treasure map, on which you display images that illustrate your management vision. A vision board is created by simply cutting out images or quotes from magazines or books and gluing them on a piece of paper or cardboard, creating a collage. By displaying either your written vision or your vision board in a prominent location, you will have a constant reminder that will help you achieve your dreams and goals.

Your managerial vision statement can also change over time, depending upon what is happening in your life and career, but many components remain consistent over time. Be sure to keep your vision clear on your management journey, but also be delighted by your discoveries along the way.

One of your first discoveries will probably be the significant change from your individual contributor role to becoming a manager of people.

Making the Transition

Part of becoming a manager is looking at things in a different way. As a manager you will act differently, deal with work issues differently, and even think differently. Making the transition means developing the three C's of Management: Confidence, Competence, and Courage.

- **Confidence** to perform your management role while being true to your vision.

- **Competence** in using your skills and abilities to perform your role, while continuing to seek opportunities for continued improvement.

- **Courage** to make the right decisions and not just the popular decisions.

Moving from an individual contributor to a manager creates changes along several spectrums, including:

From...	To...
• Be a follower ...	Be a leader
• Carry out decisions...	Make decisions
• Have a buffer ...	Be a buffer
• Work in a safe place...	Create a safe pace
• Perform to standards...	Develop standards

- Do the work yourself...   Delegate work
- Utilize your skills...   Teach skills

The job change from individual contributor to manager may seem as if it occurs instantly, with no time to adjust. On Friday you were on the team, "one of the guys," so to speak. On Monday you are the manager of the team. This situation is very typical and presents a number of interpersonal challenges as you interact with your team members. You have been given the responsibility and the power of authority based on your position. Although you have this power, you may not be quite sure how to handle it. Here are a few traps many new managers may experience:

- **Carrot and Stick:** Many managers believe that to get their team members to do something they must either offer an incentive (a carrot) or threaten them (a stick). It is important to remember that as their manager you have the power and authority and can merely ask your team in a respectful way to get the work done. There is an implicit understanding that when a manager asks for an assignment to be completed, it must be done.

- **Apologetic:** If managers are uncomfortable with their authority, it may lead them to apologize when giving assignments. There really is no reason to apologize in this case because as a manager one of your roles is to delegate work and assign duties and responsibilities. Your team members might see your apologies as lack of confidence. Simply use a professional tone of voice and provide a good

explanation; your authority to give the assignment is
inherent in your title.

- **Buddy and Pal:** Buddy and Pal behaviors typically
  occur when new managers are promoted from within
  the same department where they previously worked
  as frontline employees. You may have gone to lunch
  with the same group of people for years and even
  shared hobbies outside of work. You don't have to
  give up your friends, but the relationship may need to
  change slightly. As a manager, you are privy to
  confidential information that cannot be shared with
  others. Also, if you treat your friends differently from
  the rest of your team members there may be a
  perception of favoritism, which will impact trust in
  your department. You may want to branch out of
  your old circle by going to lunch with your fellow
  managers. It may be helpful to have a private
  discussion with friends in your department and ask
  for their cooperation in your new assignment. True
  friends will adapt to the change and do everything to
  support you in your new role.

- **Do-it-Myself:** You may have been promoted because
  you had the best skills in the department. The trap
  this presents is the tendency to want to continue to
  do the work yourself. You may have thoughts such
  as "By the time I tell him how to do it, I can do it
  myself," or "If I want this done right, I must do it
  myself." The long-term consequence of always doing
  it yourself is your team members will not have the
  opportunity to develop their skills. In addition your
  team members may not take the initiative because
  they know you will just take over the task. Doing the

work that should be done by your team members also doesn't allow you time to develop your new managerial skills.

If you find yourself in one of these traps, don't worry, you are not the first manager to encounter them on the management journey. With this new awareness, you can begin to climb out of the typical new manager trap and take positive action to substitute other behaviors and become the role model you envision.

Being a Role Model

True role models are those who possess the qualities that we admire and who have affected us in a way that make us want to be better. We've all had good managers and bad managers. You may have had managers who encouraged and inspired you and made you believe that you could accomplish anything, or you may have had managers who were screamers and disrespectful to their employees.

We can learn from both types of managers, although obviously screaming at your team members is not the way to go! You can take the best characteristics from all the managers you've met and avoid their negative characteristics to build the management role model you would like to become.

> *"Words to live by are just words unless you live by them. You have to walk the talk."*
>
> ~Eric Harvey and Al Lucia, co-authors, *Walk the Talk*

Managers are never truly off the clock because they are representatives of the company. Once you have developed your vision of what you represent as a manager, it is important to live that vision. Whether you call it modeling the way, practicing what you preach, or walking the talk, being a role model for what you believe leads to confidence, competence, and courage.

It is important, however, to be true to ourselves. We can admire strengths in others and study other great manager role models, but to be happy and successful in life means accepting who you are and what you have to offer. Your strengths can be used to develop your management style. Staying true to your strengths will make your style even more authentic. Wouldn't you like to work for an authentic manager?

Behavioral or personality profiles provide information to help you understand yourself and others. The feedback you receive from these profiles will indicate your preferred style at work. The profile assessment tool I like to use is **DiSC®** by Inscape Publishing; however, there are many other excellent profile choices. Your style may reveal one or more of the following:

- You are the type of person who is goal oriented, direct, and makes quick decisions.

- You have a style that is optimistic, very at ease in communicating, and you enjoy participating in a group.

- Your style preference may be to help others, preferring a harmonious environment and valuing cooperation.

- You are the type of person who focuses on doing things right, planning ahead, and you value privacy.

Your behavior style also impacts how you prefer to manage. Your natural behavior tendencies will impact your management preferences related to how you communicate, plan, give direction, and provide coaching.

All managers share the need to develop managerial competencies. When you utilize a management approach that fits your preferred style, you will find managing more rewarding as you develop your competence.

Managerial Competencies

The word competency is a form of the word "competence," which is the ability to perform a task. Managerial competencies are therefore the abilities, traits, and knowledge that managers need in order to be effective in their roles. Competencies are usually developed over time as we develop "competence" in our managerial role.

> *"It is my hope that competencies will provide us with shared language for talking, in concrete terms, about high performance and managerial excellence. I believe that a shared view of the standards we are striving to achieve will assist us in our continuing efforts to prepare the Organization to meet the challenges of the 21st century."*
>
> ~Kofi Annan, United Nations Secretary-General

Your organization may have developed a set of core competencies that apply to every position or for each type of position.

Here are a few examples of managerial competencies that you will find described in other chapters. Depending on the role you have, some of these competencies will be more important than others. As you review the list, you can think about your competence in each of these areas, and if they are critical for your current position.

- Administering policies and procedures
- Implementing the company vision, mission and objectives
- Building relationships with your team members
- Collaborating with other line and staff positions
- Setting goals and expectations
- Coaching your team members
- Communicating and listening

- Managing your time, planning, and prioritizing
- Understanding employment law
- Solving problems
- Managing change
- Resolving conflict

Depending on your managerial style strengths, some of the competencies will probably be easier to develop than others. But the good news is you can develop skills in all these areas. Training classes, in the form of in-person workshops and e-learning courses, are available on just about any topic.

Creating a Development Plan

What actions are you going to take to achieve your managerial vision?

> *"Vision without action is merely a dream. Action without vision just passes the time. Vision with action can change the world."*
>
> ~Joel Arthur Barker, futurist and author

You have a vision about what type of manager you want to be, and you've identified your strengths and reviewed a list of competencies. You can now create a development plan to start you on your management journey. What will you do first? What classes will you take? What books will you read? What coaching will you ask for? Here are a few questions to get you started on creating a development plan:

1. What does my organization need from its managers now and in the future?

2. What are the competencies for my position?

3. What are my current competency strengths and needs?

4. Where do I want to be in my management journey in one, two, three, four and five years?

5. How can I capitalize on my strengths?

6. What else do I need to know to be a great manager?

Developmental opportunities can take many forms, and do not necessarily just involve training. At the end of this book is a bibliography of other books to consider adding to your library. Besides formal training in a classroom setting, you can consider:

- Independent reading and research

- Starting a book club with other managers

- Shadowing a successful manager

- E-learning through the Internet or your company's intranet

- Volunteering for an assignment on a cross-functional project team

You will learn more about goal setting in Chapter Five, "Setting Your Course and Speed."

Summary

You can plan how you want to travel on your management journey by developing a managerial vision. When you utilize and are true to your natural talents, you will manage with authenticity. A development plan will assist you in increasing your confidence, competence, and courage to be a great manager.

Building Your Map
Follow-up Activities

1) Create your management vision. Check the questions you will consider; add other questions:

☐ What two to three things must be present in your environment to feel fulfilled in your work?

_____

☐ What are five to six of your most important values?

_____

☐ When your management career is ending, what will you regret not doing, seeing, or achieving?

_____

☐ What strengths do you see in yourself? What have others said about your strengths?

_____

☐ What does your environment look like?

_____

☐ What are you doing and saying?

_____

☐ What are other people doing and saying?

_____

☐ What successes are you celebrating?

_____

☐ What are your facial expression, and body language as you interact with your team members?

_____

☐ How do other people describe you?

_____

☐ _____

☐ _____

☐ _____

2)   Consider the following traps. Identify if you fall into any of these and take steps to steer away from the trap.

☐ Carrot and Stick

☐ Apologetic

☐ Buddy and Pal

☐ Do-it-Myself

3) Take a behavior style assessment such as DiSC®. Celebrate your strengths.

4) Begin your development plan.

Where to Go From Here
Helpful Training Topics

☐ Visioning skills

☐ New manager training

☐ DiSC® or other behavior style training

☐ Goal setting

TWO

NAVIGATING COMPANY EXPECTATIONS

Chapter Learning Points:
- Collect reference material to create your management guidebook
- Understand your organization's expectation of your management role

> *"I believe success is preparation, because opportunity is going to knock on your door sooner or later but are you prepared to answer that?"*
>
> ~Omar Epps, actor and musician

The World of Management

You have entered the world of management. Which way should you go? Where are the best roads, the optimal route to your destination? Do you want to travel by a direct route or take a detour to explore the countryside? It's time to get out your map and do a little navigating. But wait... Where is the map? Your management map doesn't look like a traditional map with clearly marked roads, highways, and borders. Each manager must collect information to build his or her own map.

19

Building your management map is like packing for a vacation or trip. What did you do the last time you planned a trip? You might have checked the Internet for the latest conditions, packed appropriate clothing and guidebooks for the area, and remembered a camera. If you were going skiing, you would have packed ski clothes, skis, and goggles. Camping trips would have included tents, hiking shoes, and maybe fishing licenses. A beach vacation usually requires sunscreen, swimsuits, towels, and snorkel gear.

What do all these things have in common? They are items you need to make your trip more enjoyable. You know what activities you plan to do and you bring those items that will enable you to get the most enjoyment while you participate. The right clothes, tools, and guidebooks not only make sense but increase your likelihood of enjoying your trip.

Creating Your Management Guidebook

Travel guidebooks offer advice on things to know before you go. They contain maps, history, recommended reading on the area, sightseeing tips, regional dictionaries, and more. People read travel guides before they go on trips to become familiar with the new surroundings they will be visiting. Travel guidebooks and maps are also used to recall information pertinent to a destination area. What was the recommended restaurant mentioned near that monument again? What was the word for thank you in the local language? What road is the quickest way to the highway?

Having a management travel guidebook also helps you prepare for things you might need to know. Keeping it as "ready reference" at your fingertips will help you quickly recall the information when the situation calls for it.

Whether you prefer to keep a hard copy book or maintain the information electronically, here are items to consider collecting when developing your own management travel guide:

1. Policy documents; either paper or online intranet links

2. Department procedure manuals, including safety manuals

3. Contact information for key individuals

4. Budget for your department, including salary guidelines

5. Job descriptions

6. The vision, mission, values, and objectives for your organization

7. Specific goals for your department

8. Planning tools

9. Reference books including: a dictionary, thesaurus, grammar, and business writing

1. **Policy Documents**

The purposes of policies or employee handbooks are many and include:

- Welcoming the new employee

- Listing the company's expectations for employees

- Informing employees of the benefits the company provides

- Sharing information about the company's background

Why do managers need to know the policies? Quite simply, they are the people who are responsible for administering the policies. Think about when you joined your company. The human resources department probably conducted an orientation that included key policies or an employee handbook. Many folks never look at the policies again after orientation. It is important for managers to have access to the most current version of the employee handbook and other policies in order to answer questions and to administer policies on a consistent basis.

Many questions that your team members will ask can be answered by the employee handbook. Questions such as, When can I take vacation? Can I use the company computer for personal use? Can I use my sick days for family situations? etc.

You may have questions yourself that can be answered by reviewing the handbook or policies. Do you know the holidays that are observed? Would you know what to do if someone complained about sexual harassment? Do you know the types of conduct that would result in disciplinary action?

Knowing the policies and where you can look up relevant details will make you feel more confident that you are doing the right thing and are giving the right answers to your team.

2. Department Procedure Manuals

Policies and employee handbooks tend to be general in nature and targeted to the entire employee population. In addition to the company's policy manual, each department may have its own procedure manuals containing relevant information for those working in that department.   This information is sometimes referred to as "standard operating procedures."

Procedures are designed to create consistency in completing assignments and list the company's expectations for how job duties are to be performed. They may also contain quality standards and step-by-step processes. Procedures may be hard copy manuals or information accessed through an intranet-based shared drive.

Safety manuals are more important in some industries than others and will include specific safety guidelines for equipment or procedures for the jobs in your department, as well as a list of the required safety gear, or protective equipment that your employees must utilize.

Managers will want to have any procedure manuals as a reference to understand the expectations for the department and to aid in their coaching of employees.

3. Contact Information

Your key contacts include your manager, team members, peers, vendors, and customers.

Who do you contact for computer issues? Who are your key customers? Which vendors do you contact often? If you had a quick question for one of your team members, do you have his or her phone extension? Creating a ready reference with everyone's office number, mobile number, and e-mail address allows you to find the information you need quickly and efficiently.

Where you keep the information is a matter of personal preference, but keep in mind that you may need to access it wherever you are, which may not be your office. If you do keep information on a portable tool such as a PDA (personal digital assistant), your IT department will be able to advise you of data security guidelines.

4. Budget

Some managerial positions have budget authority and some do not. A budget is a method of control to ensure decisions are made within specific parameters. The budget may include what you can spend on office supplies, equipment, travel, recognition, salaries, and raises. You may also have a budget for revenue-generating activities.

Managers will want to know the answers to these questions and others: How do I purchase needed equipment for my department? How much can I spend? When can I give an employee a raise?   Is there a required paper or online form to submit the increase? What expenses are reimbursable on business trips and which are not?   What is my authority for spending money on recognition rewards for my team members?

A salary budget can be in the form of a merit budget for the year. You may also have a pool of money for promotions. If you understand the process and approval authority for raises, you won't get into the difficult position of making promises that you can't deliver.

Budgets may be established for ordering office supplies and equipment, overtime, travel, recognition and rewards, etc. It is important to know the maximum dollar amount you can approve and what amount requires higher level approval. For example, you can order pens without approval but must submit a capital expenditure request for a new computer.

If you don't have a formal budget, you will probably at least have an outline of what your authority level is on different expense categories and which items must be submitted for approval.   For this section of your management guide you can include your budget, policies or procedures that outline how to submit expenses, and the required paper or online forms.

5. Job Descriptions

A job description provides an organization with the opportunity to describe its general expectations of an employee. A job description describes the position's duties and responsibilities. It may also include background, qualifications, and physical requirements for the job. Formalizing job descriptions is a method of organizing workflow and reducing confusion and conflict.

Job descriptions will assist you in answering such questions as: What are the job titles in my department? What are the overall purposes of the positions in my department? How are the tasks distributed among my team members? What qualifications are required to perform the jobs?

Preferring a more flexible approach, some organizations don't have formal job descriptions. In some companies, job descriptions are created for frontline employees but aren't formalized for managers. If descriptions exist for the positions in your department, however, you will want to have them as a ready reference. If your company doesn't have descriptions, just go with the flow. The most important thing is that you know the tasks your department will be responsible for completing.

Begin with collecting job descriptions for all positions and reviewing them for accuracy. Check when they were last updated; they may need to be changed. Ask your manager: "Are you aware of any changes in the process or technology that should be reflected in the current job descriptions?" You can check with job incumbents to get their perceptions of what is documented versus what they are actually doing. If rewrites are needed, usually it is the human resources department that assists you with this project.

6. Vision, Mission, Values, and Objectives

Having information on your organization's vision, mission, values, and objectives will assist you in answering questions such as: Why does my company exist? What does it want to achieve? What products and services does it offer? How does it offer its products and services?

Some companies will have these statements framed in the lobby or listed on their website. In other companies you may have to read the strategic plan to locate them. Not all companies take the time to establish all of the above, but your company has, it is important to know what they are and what they mean to you and your department.

Here are a few definitions:

A **vision statement** outlines what a company wants to be. It focuses on tomorrow, it is inspirational, and it provides clear, decision-making criteria. Picture the rainbow over a mountaintop with a pot of gold at its end.

A **mission statement** outlines the purpose of the company or why it exists. It focuses on today and usually includes what products and services it supplies, the customer type, and how it supplies products and services. Mission statements tend to be more practical than vision statements and should be what people recite when asked, "What does your company do?"

Values are behavior-guiding principles that employees are expected to follow in making decisions and carrying out their duties and responsibilities. Examples include integrity, innovation, customer focus, and teamwork.

Objectives are results that an organization seeks to achieve in pursuing its basic mission.   Long-term objectives are established for three-to five-year period. Short-term objectives are created for six months to one year. Objectives should be updated at least every year, depending on internal and external factors.

Your manager is a great resource to assist you in interpreting how these statements impact your department. You will then be the resource for your team members so they can understand how their individual jobs impact the company.

7. Specific Goals for Your Department

Most organizations conduct goal-setting sessions at least annually. Understanding the goals of the organization will assist you to align what your department needs to accomplish within the overall strategy.

Collecting your department goals will answer the following questions: What will my department need to achieve this year? What are our top priorities?   What measurements are in place? How will accomplishing our goals contribute to the organization's strategic plan?

See Chapter Five, "Setting Your Course and Speed" to learn more about goal setting.

8. Planning Tools

Managers are always planning. To-do lists to capture your most important tasks of the day as well as a calendar for scheduling are critical tools for every manager. There are many paper, online, and electronic planning tools available for every preference. What is the best planning tool? The tool that you will use!

9. Reference Books

As a manager, you will often be required to create written documents. There are many online reference sources that will help you write professionally. Many managers find it useful to have copies of reference books available; however, the actual source is a matter of personal preference.

- **Dictionary**: This reference book not only assists you with spelling, but gives additional information for each word, including meaning, pronunciation, and etymology.

- **Thesaurus**: A book of synonyms that expands the vocabulary you use in your writing by providing you with variety of word choices.

- **Grammar**: A good reference to review capitalization, punctuation, sentence construction, and word usage rules. For example, do you remember the difference between affect and effect? How about advice and advise? Keeping a grammar reference on hand will aid you in your professional writing.

- **Business writing**: As a manager you often will be required to write various letters, reports, and documents. What does your writing style say about you? A good reference book will help you improve the clarity and professionalism of your writing.

Asking for Directions Along the Way

Collecting the information listed above puts you well underway in creating a management guidebook that will be an invaluable reference tool during your journey.

As you collected the information you may have struggled a bit in locating some items and had to ask for assistance from others. Being willing to ask for directions and read the "road signs" on your management journey will enable you to achieve your management vision much more quickly.

Many of you may have worked for years in the department you now supervise or manage. You may be thinking, "I don't need to stop for directions, I know how it's done. I know our goals, that is why they promoted me because I know where I'm going and the best way to get there." If you weren't good at your job and confident in your abilities, you probably wouldn't be in your new position right now. Consider the possibility that although you knew the best way to get things done from your old position and point of view, you probably don't know the best way to get there from a management point of view.

Have you ever flown in a plane over your neighborhood? If you look closely you will recognize the parks and lakes you have driven by countless times and perhaps even your own home. Things look very different from 10,000 feet up in the air, don't they?

Now that you are a manager, things will also look different. Confidence in your abilities is great, but having the courage to ask questions and for directions is important too.

I've seen many managers get frustrated in their new roles. They say, "I'm working long hours and knocking myself out, but my manager never seems to appreciate it." What is usually the case is that the new managers are working hard but on the wrong things. The managers are doing the things they think need to be done instead of focusing on what the company expects them to do.

The Expectations Meeting

As soon as possible, schedule a meeting with your manager to discuss his or her goals and expectations for you and your department. Scheduling the meeting instead of just "dropping by" allows your manager to have the time to focus on giving you the directions you need without either of you feeling rushed. Scheduling the meeting will also give your manager a chance to prepare and collect information.

You may wish to bring all or some of the information you collected for your management guidebook for discussion or clarification. For example, you could share your department goals to obtain your manager's input. Your manager may completely change your plans, adjust them slightly, or happily approve them, but any of these is terrific news. It's terrific because you would now be headed in the right direction. Isn't it better to be headed in the right direction than to think "I'm making great progress, look how far down the road I am," only to find out you are going down the wrong road?

> *"If you don't know where you're going, any road will take you there."*
>
> ~Lewis Carroll, English author

Here are a few potential agenda items for your expectations meeting:

1. What your manager sees as the key challenges for you and your department

2. How your performance and the performance of your team will be measured

3. The communication preferences of your manager

4. Your manager's "hot buttons"

These items are provided as a checklist and don't necessarily need to be discussed in this order you can skip around depending on how the conversation flows.

1. Key Challenges

In identifying the key challenges from your manager's point of view, you are getting in sync with the direction you need to take and are spending time on the things that matter most.

Begin by clarifying the goals and objectives for your department with your manager.

Suggested questions you can use for this part of the discussion include:

- What do you see as our key challenges this year?
- What are the top three things you would like the department to accomplish this year?
- What should be our primary focus in accomplishing our goals?
- Are there any barriers you foresee for us in accomplishing our goals?
- Do you have any recommendations on how we can overcome the barriers?
- What are the personal development goals you would like me to work on this year?

Getting this information at the beginning of your journey clarifies your direction and roads to take, which is important to know before you get started. It is important to put the final goal outcomes in writing to ensure mutual understanding with your manager.

2. How Performance Will Be Measured

This topic goes together nicely with your goals. Your performance will be measured based on what you and your department accomplishes; the end result. It may also be measured on a collection of behaviors that assist in accomplishing your goals.

Most organizations have performance appraisal programs and related forms. For managers, the forms usually have a "management-by-objectives" section, which lists the specific goals for the time period. Another common section is "behavior expectations." Examples of items in this section include: quality, customer orientation, teamwork, and decision making.

Another item to include in your management travel guidebook is a copy of the performance appraisal forms for your position and your team members' positions. They may be the same or they may be different. Your company may have an online form instead of a printed document, or a form may not exist. But if it has one, it is important to know what it is, when it must be completed, and how it should be completed.

Suggested questions you can use for this part of the discussion are:

- How will we know that our department is accomplishing our key objectives?

- What measurements are in place that coincides with our goals?

- Can you provide me with examples of the critical behaviors you would like to see in my department?

- Are there specific things you would like me to keep in mind when I complete performance appraisals?

Many department managers get frustrated when they complete performance appraisals for the first time and their manager disagrees with how the employees have been rated, either too high or too low. It is much better to clarify performance expectations up front.

3. Communication Preferences

Every individual has different preferences, especially when it involves frequency and types of communication. Your manager's style has a lot to do with his or her preferences and how best to interact with him or her. It is usually best not to assume that you and your manager have the same preferences.

Suggested questions you can use for this part of the discussion would include:

- How often would you like me to communicate with you: daily, weekly or monthly?

- What communication method would you prefer: over the phone, in person, by e-mail, or text message?

- What level of detail would you like in my communications? Do you want bottom line results or specific details?

- How often would you like an update on goal accomplishments?

- Do you have regularly scheduled meetings with your direct reports? When and where are the meetings? What expectations do you have for meeting participants?

You may also want to think about what your communication preferences are to share with your manager.

4. Your Manager's "Hot Buttons"

Hot buttons are those irritations and annoyances that can cause frustration and sometimes conflict. Examples include: not receiving notice on changes, being late for meetings, interruptions, and disorganized communication.

Everyone has a hot button. You know when you've accidently hit it when the level of irritation increases in the individual. The more you know about a person's preferences, the more you can adapt your style to theirs and avoid hitting a hot button.

Some managers may be irritated by indecision, by routine and excessive detail, by impatience or insensitivity, or by unpredictability and too short deadlines.

So how to you find out about hot buttons? Observation is one way. You can read nonverbal clues such as body language or facial expression to look for irritation or annoyance. You may have picked up clues during your expectations meeting or previous interactions with your manager. Or you can just ask your manager about what causes irritations. Here is a question you can use for this part of the discussion:

Is there anything I should know about how you like to work and your behavior expectations for the members of your team that we haven't discussed yet?

You've created a management travel guidebook and you've had an expectations meeting with your manager to ensure you are on the right path on your management journey. There is only one thing left on your packing list; the right clothes.

Clothes for Your Journey

We probably would all agree how odd it would look to be dressed in a ski parka on a 90-degree day at the beach or in formal attire on a hiking trail. Besides the comfort factor, people will look at you strangely and wonder: "What's the matter with that guy? Didn't he know we were going hiking today?"

Newly promoted managers also make mistakes in the image they present. It is important to recognize that the environment and journey have changed, and what was appropriate attire as an individual contributor may not be right for a management position. People may be thinking: "What is the matter with that guy? Doesn't he know he's a manager now?"

Every company has its own standard of dress, just like every company has its own culture. Some industries such as banking may be more formal, and others like advertising may be more casual. The term "business casual" can mean different things in different companies. Business casual also means different things to different people, and sometimes can be misinterpreted.

A high school student was going on his first interview. His mother said to him, "Larry, aren't you going to put shoes on for your interview?" He said: "I do have shoes on!" They were athletic shoes. When his mother explained the type of shoes he should be wearing, he had a horrified look on his face as he said, "You mean I have to wear those uncomfortable things?"

You'll need to know your company's dress code to be able to coach your employees on proper attire and you will also want to be seen as a role model and not violate the policy. The policy is usually written by the human resources department, so visiting with them to clarify requirements and how to administer the dress code policy is a good first step.

The next step is to observe how other managers dress in your company. Look at everything including cloth- ing, accessories, and shoes. Notice things like color, style, fit, length, etc. You may have to start shopping in new type of store to locate clothing items not currently in your closet. You may also want to observe how the next level of management dresses. It never hurts to start dressing toward a position for the future!

Dressing for business these days has also become situational. Visiting clients or interviewing a candidate may require more professional attire. Some managers I know keep a professional blazer in a neutral shade in their office in case they need to attend an unexpected meeting.

Summary

Managers can pack for their journey by creating a management travel guidebook with key information. Being prepared with information at your fingertips will increase your confidence and competence as a manager. Your manager is a terrific source for company expectations for your role and performance, therefore it is important to keep communication lines open.

Building Your Map
Follow-Up Activities

1) Create a written and/or virtual guidebook.
Check which items you will include; add your own items:

☐ Policy manuals, including the employee handbook

☐ Department procedure manuals

☐ Contact information for key individuals

☐ Budget for your department, including salary guidelines

☐ Job descriptions

☐ Mission, vision, values, and objectives

☐ Specific goals for your department

☐ Planning tools

☐ A dictionary, thesaurus, grammar, and writing reference books

☐ _____

☐ _____

☐ _____

2) Hold an expectations meeting with your manager. Check which topics you will include; add your own topics:

☐ What your manager sees as the key challenges for you and your department

☐ How your performance and the performance of your team will be measured

☐ The communication preferences of your manager

☐ Your manager's "hot buttons"

☐ _____

☐ _____

☐ _____

3) Review your wardrobe, comparing it with what other managers wear as well as your company dress code.

Where to Go From Here
Helpful Training Topics

☐ Interviewing skills
☐ Communication skills

THREE

GETTING TO KNOW YOUR TRAVELING COMPANIONS

Chapter Learning Points:
- Gather information about your team members
- Understand team member expectations

"No road is long with good company."

~Turkish proverb

Improving Your Journey

Congratulations! You have just won a trip to Hawaii, all expenses paid! The only catch is you have to go with people you've never met. Can you imagine going on a vacation with people you don't know? What impact would that have on your enjoyment of the trip?

You probably would be concerned about whether your traveling companions were early or late risers. You might be wondering if they enjoy the same activities as you do or even the same food. Are you a surfer and scuba diver or would you rather see the sites from the comfort of a tour bus? How would knowing more about your traveling companions improve the journey?

Of course it would improve your journey tremendously; after all, we choose our vacation traveling companions based on who shares our likes and dislikes. Even if you travel with family members who don't always share your interests, at least you know each other and can compromise during your vacation so everyone has a good time.

Management is not an independent journey. If this is your first management position, you have moved from an independent contributor to a manager of people. The team members you manage are your new traveling companions. Sometimes you can choose your team members, but often your traveling companions are chosen for you. Getting to know your team members will lead to more enjoyment of the journey for everyone. Each of your team members will have their own expectations, goals, fears, motivations, and approaches to work.

Many managers make the mistake of just assuming they know all about their team members and their team knows them. Most people assume that everyone else acts, thinks, and feels like they do. But just like some folks enjoy surfing and others like touring in an air-conditioned bus, everyone's work expectation preferences are different.

Team Member Expectations

> *"Expectation is the engine that drives satisfaction. All satisfaction or dissatisfaction is the result of a gap between expectations and reality."*
>
> ~Nicholas DiMarco, professor, Webster University

An expectation is what your team members assume they should receive in return for what they contribute at work. Your team members have expectations about their work environment. For example, teamwork may be important for some folks and for others, autonomy must be present for them to feel satisfied at work. Career growth may be an important expectation for your team members, or they may have a preference for a stable work environment.

Why are managers concerned about knowing employee expectations? When expectations are not met they lead to:

- Negative attitudes
- Decreased job satisfaction
- Decreased productivity
- Increased turnover

The key to understanding expectations is to ask about them in a discussion with your team members. You may be thinking, "What if I can't meet their expectations? Will I make the situation worse by asking for expectations, and then not being able to meet them?"

Even if you can't accommodate someone's expectation, it is better to at least openly discuss it. An unspoken expectation may make team members resentful, especially if they believe their manager should know what they expect. Uncovering expectations gives a manager an opportunity to determine if there are any changes that can be made to meet those expectations. Employees will appreciate that their manager took the initiative to find out what was important to them and made an effort, even if it can't be done.

Let's take an example. Fiona joined a large accounting firm as a tax accountant before she married into a large family that enjoys doing a variety of activities together. Work/life flexibility has become a new workplace expectation for Fiona. Her manager had an "expectation discussion" about what was important to Fiona on the job. The outcome of the discussion was that her job during tax season is very demanding and requires most of her time and focus, but the rest of the year her manager is willing to provide more scheduling flexibility. Fiona also volunteered during the discussion to speak to her husband about taking on more responsibility at home during tax season so her free time could be spent on the activities they enjoy with their family. By communicating in an open discussion, Fiona was able to achieve more of the work/life flexibility she needed and her manager was able to understand more about Fiona's expectations.

The "getting-to-know-you" meeting is one way to learn about what your team members expect.

The "Getting-to-Know-You" Meeting

This meeting helps you get ahead of the curve by getting to know each of your employees, building trust, and finding out their preferences *before* major roadblocks occur.

Some of your employees may be exactly like you; others may have an entirely different style or opposite expectations. What is the best way to find out? Ask them! You may want to prepare answers to the following questions so you can share things about yourself during the discussion. Remember, your employees also need to know you as a traveling companion. Here are some key questions:

1. **What is your preferred style at work?**

2. **What form of communication do you prefer?**

3. **How do you like to be recognized?**

4. **What do you like/dislike about the work you do?**

5. **What do you like about the work environment and what would you change?**

6. **What are your future goals and what additional training would you like?**

7. **Is there anything else you want me, as your manager, to know about you?**

1. What is your preferred style at work?

As mentioned previously, there are quite a few behavior style assessments available. Talking about behavior styles at work is a great way to improve communication and teamwork by supplying a common language. People may have one preferred style or several. Although my preference is the **DiSC**® Profile by Inscape Publishing, if your company uses another behavior/personality assessment, you can use that common language to start your discussion.

The purpose of sharing work styles is to gain greater insight into how to utilize everyone's strengths and understand the best way to work together. It is important that different styles are seen as just that – different – and not wrong.

Knowing your own style and sharing it with your team members will allow you to compare where you may see eye-to-eye and where there may be points of potential conflict.

> *"Do Unto Others As They Would Have You Do Unto Them."*
>
> ~Dr. Tony Alessandra, author, *The Platinum Rule*®

2. What form of communication do you prefer?

Some folks like e-mail, and others are almost fused to their PDA (personal digital assistant) and may think meetings are a waste of time. Others like the interaction that verbal communication provides and find written communication too impersonal. Discuss how you plan to communicate with the team and ask for their feedback and preferences. Chapter 6, "Opening Communication Channels" provides more information on communication methods.

3. How do you like to be recognized?

Recognition contributes to job satisfaction, promotes involvement, raises morale, and inspires loyalty. Many employees complain about a lack of recognition in the workplace. Even companies that have formal recognition systems in place sometimes hear this feedback. The explanation may be that it's the wrong type of recognition or they don't receive the recognition from the right person. Quite often it's the simple pat on the back, hearing your name mentioned at a company meeting, or a sincere thank you from your manager that is important. Public recognition is terrific for some people, others may be embarrassed by this and prefer a one-on-one compliment. "Just send me an e-mail" may be a third response to this question.

4. What do you like about the work you do? What do you dislike? How can this activity be changed to make it better for you?

This is a great way to get to know your team members' preferences. It may not seem possible to change job assignments based on what everyone likes or dislikes, but you'll never know unless you start asking questions. At the end of your "getting-to-know-you" meeting you may have found someone who likes to do what another person dislikes. Switching around job duties may lead to more overall satisfaction on the job. Another option is to examine if simple, routine tasks can be automated.

5. What do you like about the work environment and what would you change?

The work environment is more than just the physical space. The environment can also involve the amount of formality, structure, organization, communication, friendliness, teamwork, etc. This question leads to a discussion about expectations. Another way to rephrase this question is, "What motivates you about our workplace and what demotivates you?"

6. What are your future goals? How can I help you achieve your goals? What additional training would you like?

If you understand your employees' goals, you can encourage attendance at training classes or special assignments. It is also important to know if your employee is happy staying in his current position, so you don't push him towards another job he might dislike. If you are not sure about what training classes are available, either internally or externally, your human resources department should be able to assist you. As an example, when Tom, a customer service representative, was asked about what training he would like he answered that he would like to attend a basic Spanish class to aid in his ability to communicate with customers who do not speak English. This idea led to offering a Spanish language program for any customer contact team member who wanted to enroll. The discussion resulted in not only assisting Tom with his goals, but others in helping the company service its customers.

7. Is there anything else you want me, as your manager, to know about you?

You are not managing a person who ceases to exist at 5 pm when he or she walks out the door. To manage the whole person you need to know the whole person and what is important to him. By phrasing the question in this manner, your team member is free to bring up other aspects of the job or even talk about outside interests. If you know your team member's hobbies you can inquire about how her softball team did the previous evening, or how the piano lessons are coming along. It is important to share whatever you are comfortable with about your outside interests as well.

Having the "getting-to-know-you" meetings and truly listening to your team members is a start to building strong relationships. Following up on the information continues the relationship-building process.

At the end of the "getting-to-know-you" meeting, you can brainstorm a to-do list for yourself as well as your team member. Keeping the information available and referring to it before interacting with your team members will help you adjust to their needs, styles, and preferences. Managers who have trusting relationships with their team members greatly contribute to their company's employee retention efforts.

> *"People leave managers, not companies."*
>
> ~Marcus Buckingham and Curt Coffman, authors, *First, Break All the Rules*

The more managers can know about their team members, the more they can create an environment that will contribute to employee satisfaction and organizational productivity. A loss of a key team member impacts an organization in a number of ways:

- Lost productivity caused by an experienced team member leaving
- Lost productivity due to a vacant position
- Recruiting, interviewing, and paperwork costs
- Lost productivity to get a new team member trained
- Lost productivity of co-workers and the manager who will answer questions from the new team member

Therefore the manager's role in retention is critical. The more you know about your team members, the better you can perform this role.

Take a Snapshot of Your Team

Taking a snapshot of your team doesn't involve a camera; it is a way of learning about the composition of your work team. Do you have an experienced group or novices? Do you have long service employees or new recruits? How long has your team worked together? Is your group highly educated or will they need training?

A good way to find out about the composition of your team is to review individual personnel files. The previous manager may have kept files on the team, but most likely you will have to visit human resources to obtain the official company file.

You can create a matrix to collect a snapshot of your team's background and experience by listing everyone's name down the side of the page and at the top list things such as:

- Years with the company
- Years in current position
- Years of outside company experience
- Education level
- Certifications
- Special skills
- Last performance evaluation score

Your matrix will reveal the overall experience and skills of your whole team. You may be surprised to learn of special skills that aren't being utilized by your team members.

Summary

Your team members are your traveling companions on your management journey. Getting to know their styles and expectations increases the enjoyment of the journey for you and your team members. Building trusting relationships with your team members improves employee retention and morale.

Building Your Map
Follow-up Activities

1) Complete a personnel file review

2) Conduct a "getting-to-know-you" meeting with your team members. Check which questions you will ask; add your own questions:

☐ What is your preferred style at work?

☐ What form of communication do you prefer?

☐ How do you like to be recognized?

☐ What do you like/dislike about the work you do?

☐ What do you like about the work environment and what would you change?

☐ What are your future goals and what additional training would you like?

☐ Is there anything else you want me, as your manger, to know about you?

☐ _____

☐ _____

☐ _____

3) Follow up on items from your "getting-to-know-you" meetings.

Where to Go From Here
Helpful Training Topics

- ☐ Interview skills
- ☐ Listening skills
- ☐ Retention
- ☐ Expectations
- ☐ Motivation

FOUR

NO MANAGER IS AN ISLAND

Chapter Learning Points:
- Make a connection with your key contacts
- Utilize collaboration skills with your connections

> *"No man is an island, entire of itself; every man is a piece of the continent, a part of the main...."*
>
> ~John Donne, English clergyman and poet

Are You an Island or Part of an Island Chain?

It is easy to get caught up in your own department and your own team. It is almost like being on an island; you have your own "shoreline," a charted territory that is well-known by you and your team members. As a way of describing their departments, other managers may say: "This is my island, my area of control. We do a great job on my island; we have well-trained inhabitants who all care about producing our island's products and services."

The shoreline, however, will sometimes become a barrier that creates an inward focus. After your work product leaves your shores, you wave farewell and start focusing on the next activities for your island once again.

It may help to think about your island, of which you are very proud, as part of an island chain. What is most important is what the entire island chain produces, not just what your island achieves. The objective for any organization is customer satisfaction. If one department excels and another does not, the organization does not achieve its overall objective.

Consider a manufacturing company. The orders come in to the customer service department, which sends the order instructions to the manufacturing department. The product is then sent to the packaging department, which sends it to the shipping department.

If your "island" is customer service, you may be proud of the accuracy of your order taking and how prompt you get it to manufacturing. But what if it is manufactured incorrectly or shipping sends the product late or to the wrong place? Has your company truly delivered on its promise of service to the customer? The customer service island has succeeded, but the island chain has failed.

Organizations often encourage an inward focus on continuous improvement within each department. Successful organizations also encourage a teamwork outward focus between other departments and functions within the company. This lets everyone understand the whole value chain of their products and services from the customer point of view. Remember that view of your home from 10,000 feet? The ability to see the "big picture" contributes to customer satisfaction. Each department or function adds value toward the end result; each link in the chain must be strong.

Collaborating with Neighboring Islands

Who is part of your island chain? You can start by making a list of other departments, especially those that perform key functions or those you interact with the most frequently. Then it is a matter of building a "collaboration bridge" to neighboring islands.

> *"Teamwork is the ability to work together toward a common vision. The ability to direct individual accomplishments toward organizational objectives. It is the fuel that allows common people to attain uncommon results."*
>
> ~Andrew Carnegie, industrialist and philanthropist

Why should you collaborate with your peers? It may help to make a list of your goals so that you can see how having a stronger relationship with other departments would help you achieve your goals. But that would be only half the story. It is important to learn the goals and objectives of other departments to see things from their points of view. How will collaborating more with you help *them* achieve success?

Behavior on the job is driven by how people are measured and rewarded. You are very familiar with the measurements for your department and how your performance will be rewarded. Do you know how other departments are measured and rewarded? The key to collaborating is to find out what other departments need from you so everyone succeeds.

Which is the better collaboration approach? Someone who approaches you by saying, "I think if you work closer with me, I will better be able to achieve my goals this year, or someone who says, "I think if we work together we'll both benefit, I'd like to hear more about your goals this year?" The second statement takes the focus away from you and places it on the other person's needs.

> *"Walls turned sideways are bridges."*
>
> ~Angela Davis, political activist and university professor

Roadside Assistance from Support Departments

Just about every medium to large organization has departments that support running the business. These departments perform activities that are usually called staff functions. They include accounting/finance, human resources and information technology (IT). Staff functions differ from line functions in that they are responsible for providing advice, research and support to the departments that accomplish the company's primary objectives.

Folks from staff departments can be considered "roadside assistance" on your management journey. They have in-depth skills and experience that you can call upon when needed. Just like gas stations, auto repair shops, tire retailers, etc. help you on a road journey, this organizational roadside assistance advice will be invaluable during your management journey.

Need help with a complex people issue? Call on your human resources department. Need to utilize a computer program to improve productivity? Call your IT department.

In a business setting, sometimes roadside assistance doesn't wait for you but arrives on your doorstep to offer advice. The human resource manager may offer advice on how to improve and complete your performance appraisals; the controller may provide instructions on how to maintain your budget. Rather than seeing these people as intrusions on your day when they offer unsolicited advice, you can reframe this point of view by seeing the value they bring to the organization.

Having professionals with specialized knowledge at their fingertips improves the efficiency and effectiveness of the organization, and also ensures regulatory compliance. For example, when your IT department requires that all software be approved by them before it is added to computers, they are preventing potential copyright violations and a possible virus attack to your whole computer network.

Building a collaboration bridge to staff functions can be just as beneficial as your collaboration bridges to the departments that perform line functions. To help in building the bridge, consider the following:

- Identify how improving interaction with the staff functions will benefit your department.

- Find out the goals and objectives of the staff functions.

- Ask how you can work together to achieve results for everyone.

How to Build a Strong Collaboration Bridge

Collaborating with others requires building trusting relationships. Several ways to build trust include:

- **Keeping your commitments**: Do you always do what you say you will do? Your colleagues have to trust that when you make a commitment you'll keep it. Try to establish realistic deadlines before committing.

- **Focusing on WIIFM**: WIIFM is an acronym for What's In It For Me. People are always tuned in to how the situation impacts their own goals and motivation. Successful collaborators can tune in to what's in it for the other person.

- **Engaging in problem solving**: When conflicts or misunderstandings occur between departments do you react with creative problem solving? Now that you know the other department's goals and priorities, you can try looking at it from their point of view when exploring alternatives until a win-win solution is discovered.

- **Taking initiative to share ideas**: See an article that relates to your colleague's challenges? Notice they don't receive a report that contains critical information for their departments? Take the initiative to provide ideas and information of benefit to other department managers.

- **Giving others credit for their ideas and work**: Of course the best way to *remove* trust from a business relationship is to take credit for the ideas or work of others. If someone says, "This is great. Who thought of this?" make sure the right person is recognized.

- **Adapting to their style**: Just as it is important to adapt to the style of your team members, understanding and adapting to your peer managers also makes sense. Each behavior style has a different set of preferences and requires a different way of approaching situations.

External Connections Past Your Island Chain

Take out your binoculars and gaze past your own island and the whole island chain that is your company. Who else is out there that matters? Your external connections can include customers, vendors, and even competitors.

Your company's purpose is to supply services and/or products to customers. Only companies with excellent service can remain competitive in today's business climate.

Talk to anyone about customer service these days and it won't take long to hear stories of poor service. In an effort to improve customer service, many organizations have customer feedback mechanisms. Hotels send e-mail follow-up surveys, retail stores have websites or phone numbers at the bottoms of receipts, all to capture information that will allow them to improve service. One of the most important strategies is to have customer focused employees. Part of your role as a manager is to be an advocate for customer service and create a service mindset for your team members.

> *"The single most important thing to remember about any enterprise is that there are no results inside its walls. The result of a business is a satisfied customer."*
>
> ~Peter Drucker, management theorist

Karl Albrecht and Ron Zemke coined the phrase "moments of truth" in their book *Service America!* You can help your employees identify all the "moments of truth" within their job responsibilities and learn how they can create moments of magic and not moments of misery.

Your department may not interact directly with external customers, but everyone has customers. Your customers may be internal people who in turn interact with external customers. Providing moments of magic to internal customers will assist them in improving overall customer service.

An excellent activity for you and your employees to do is have a brainstorming session answering these questions:

1. Who are our customers, both internal and external?

2. What do our customers want?

3. How do our customers benefit from our service/product?

4. What are the consequences of bad service to our customers?

5. How can we create moments of magic in every one of our interactions with our customers?

Building Bridges to Improve Vendor Relationships

As part of your managerial job, you may be required to interact with company vendors. Vendors may include a printer, a supplier of raw material, a temporary agency, etc. The good news is now you are the customer and can expect moments of magic to be delivered to you and your company.

Vendor relationships can be improved, as with any relationship, by having a two-way dialog. To receive excellent service you may have to describe what excellent service means to you by clearly explaining your expectations. You can reach out to your vendors and ask if there is any other information you can supply that will assist them in supplying the service you need.

Building a strong partnership with your vendor contacts can be very rewarding; after all, they are assisting you in achieving your goals. Your loyalty must always be to your organization, however, and not to your vendor contact. If you are not receiving the products and services you need, it may be necessary to replace the vendor. If this decision doesn't fall within your authority, it is important to let those with the responsibility know about your experiences, both good and bad.

Why Should You Know about the Competition?

Everyone has competitors. Your customers have choices on where to purchase their products and services. In the spirit of continuous improvement for your own service, it is important to see what choices are in the marketplace.

Just about everyone has a website these days, so that is a good starting point in learning about the competition. If your competitors have retail establishments, you could visit as a customer. Your customers may even mention your competitors.

After you visit your competitor's website or location, you can make a list of their strengths and weaknesses. What do you offer that they don't? What do they have that you don't? What ideas did you learn that you can now change or improve in your department?

One thing you can learn is how they treat customers. In fact, you can learn quite a bit even from companies that are not in your industry or compete with your company by putting yourself in the shoes of a customer. Since everyone is a customer, whether it's going to the grocery store, calling a utility company, shopping for clothing, or going to a restaurant, your team members can get involved in identifying good customer service.

Here are some topics for a great brainstorming session you can have with your team members:

1. Describe the last time you were a customer and received excellent service.

2. List the things the person did that made the service excellent.

3. What can we apply in our department for our external and internal customers?

4. List action steps for implementation.

Summary

Connecting with other departments as well as with your external contacts contributes to your organization's success.   Developing collaboration skills involves understanding the needs and goals of others. Involving your team members in brainstorming and planning improves service to customers both internal and external.

Building Your Map
Follow-up Activities

1) Develop a list with four columns:

a. Names of other departments and staff functions

b. Benefits of collaborating with them

c. Benefits of collaborating with you from their point of view

d. Their goals and objectives and how they are measured

2) Set up a meeting with your key contacts. Check which questions you will ask; add your own questions:

☐ How will our collaborating more assist your department?

☐ What are the goals and objectives for your department?

☐ What can my department do to assist you with your goals and objectives?

☐ _____

☐ _____

☐ _____

3) Lead a brainstorming session with your team members. Check which questions you will utilize; add your own questions:

☐ Who are our customers, both internal and external?

☐ What do our customers want?

☐ How do our customers benefit from our service/product?

☐ What are the consequences of bad service to our customers?

☐ How can we create moments of magic in every one of our interactions with our customers?

☐ _____

☐ _____

☐ _____

4) Make a list of your vendors and add your expectations. Meet with vendors to share your expectations, how they are meeting them, and what can be improved.

5) Lead a brainstorming session with your team members. Check which questions you will utilize; add your own questions:

☐ Describe the last time you were a customer and received excellent service.

☐ List the things the person did that made the service excellent.

☐ What can we apply in our department for our external and internal customers?

☐ List action steps for implementation.

☐ _____

☐ _____

☐ _____

Where to Go From Here
Helpful Training Topics

- ☐ Interview skills
- ☐ Listening skills
- ☐ Communication skills
- ☐ Facilitation skills
- ☐ Collaborating skills
- ☐ DiSC® or other behavior style training

FIVE

SETTING YOUR COURSE AND SPEED

Chapter Learning Points:
- Establish goals for your department and team
- Communicate expectations for your team members

> *"The reason most people never reach their goals is that they don't define them, or ever seriously consider them as believable or achievable. Winners can tell you where they are going, what they plan to do along the way and who will be sharing the adventure with them...."*
>
> ~Dr. Denis Waitley, author, *The Psychology of Winning*

Setting Goals for Your Journey

Let's say you have a long road trip planned that will last several days. You have a goal of reaching your destination by Friday. You've done the research, have a map, planned your route, created an itinerary, and decided when you need to leave in order to arrive on time. You've set milestones on how many miles you want to travel before stopping for gas or before lunch or by day's end. Your calculations are based on what you know about how many miles to the tank your car

71

averages, traffic patterns, the speed limit on the roadways you've planned, how long you anticipate for each stop along the way, etc. Some of your plans were based on experience and some were educated guesses based on the factors you identified. You know whether or not your plan is working because you can measure your progress by the roadside mile markers and your watch.

In examining this road trip analogy we can see the important aspects for business goal setting:

1. **Goal**: Your goal is your destination; the final result you want to accomplish at the end of the period, usually annually. The goal is typically stated with an end date. In the example above, the goal was to arrive at our final destination by Friday.

2. **Resources**: This is what you have available to accomplish your goal. Resources can be people, time, money, equipment, space, etc. Knowing the strengths and limitations of your resources assists you in developing your plan. Some of the resources we had in the road trip were our car, roadways, money for gas and food, and the accuracy of our map.

3. **Plan**: Your plan outlines how you will achieve your goal. Your plan is adjusted based on the availability of your resources. It answers the question, "How will you achieve your goal?" In order to reach our destination by Friday, we need to calculate miles to the gallon and how many

miles we can cover each day based on the speed limit. This information lets us create a plan for when to leave and when and where to stop each day.

4. **Milestones**: Interim goals during the period will indicate how close you are to your overall goal. Setting monthly or quarterly milestones will aid in achieving the desired final result. The milestones in our road trip were the number of miles covered and the stopping points reached each day.

5. **Measurements**: This answers the question "Was the goal attained?" You can also measure how much of the goal was accomplished. For example, you can state that 75% of the goal was realized. The measurement on our road trip was pretty easy; either we were at our final destination on Friday or we were not.

Your department's goals may have already been established when you received your management position, in which case you were able to collect the goals to add to your management guidebook. During your expectations meeting, you had the opportunity to clarify and finalize your goals with your manager.

But what if this is the beginning of the year or you have become a manager of a new department with no established goals? Where and how do you start?

Starting the Goal-Setting Process

> *"People with goals succeed because they know where they're going."*
>
> ~Earl Nightingale, American motivational speaker

A good place to start is the vision, mission, values, and objectives for your organization that you collected as part of your management guidebook. Cascading goals occur when your department goals reflect what the company plans to achieve, so that every department's goals cascade down from the goals above like a waterfall. What is the focus of your organization this year? Improve customer service? Increase the number of clients? Reduce turnover? Increase productivity? Understanding your organization's focus aids in developing department goals that will make a contribution to the overall goal.

Here are examples of a goal using each aspect of the goal setting process:

1. **Goal**: Achieve 80% customer satisfaction ratings by December 31st.

2. **Resources**: Customer service representatives, computer system, and money for customer service training.

3. **Plan**: Supply more information to customer service representatives who are directly on the customer order system using built-in help screens and the company's shared knowledge system.

Provide training to representatives on interpersonal and problem-solving skills. Post monthly customer satisfaction statistics.

4. **Milestones**: Place computer system upgrade request to IT by January 15th. Schedule a series of training classes to be held monthly beginning February 1st.

5. **Measurements**: Measure and display customer satisfaction statistics at the end of each month and at year end.

> *"If you have a goal in life that takes a lot of energy, that requires a lot of work, that incurs a great deal of interest and that is a challenge to you, you will always look forward to waking up to see what the new day brings."*
>
> ~Susan Polis Schultz, poet and women's activist

In addition to establishing goals for your department, you may also wish to consider specific development goals for yourself. If this is your first role as a manager, attending a management development course would be a logical target goal. A good place to start is to ask for feedback from your manager or go back and look at your last performance appraisal. Your company may offer in-house training or you may choose to enroll in a public seminar. As with your department goals, for each of your personal goals you will want to list a target date, required resources, a specific plan, milestones, and how you will measure it for completing each of your personal goals. At the end of each chapter in this book is a list of related training topics to provide you with development ideas.

You have begun the process by drafting your department and personal goals; it is now time to think about involving your team members. Your team members will need to know the goals and how they can contribute to their accomplishment. They will also have insights in what can and cannot be achieved based on their own perspectives. It is better to identify barriers and possible ways to overcome them before goals are finalized than to set unrealistic goals that won't be achieved and may demotivate you and your team.

Participative Goal Setting with Your Team

What do your employees need to know about department goals? Let's consider an example. You walk into a room and see a game on the TV. Typically, what would be your first questions?

You might ask, **Who is playing**? **What is the score?** And if it's a game you've never seen before, **How is it played?**

"The trouble with not having a goal is that you can spend your life running up and down the field and never score."

~Bill Copeland, Australian umpire

Involving your employees in goal setting involves similar questions.

1. **Who is playing?** Employees need to feel part of the team and that they can make a contribution. Retention improves when people feel they are an essential part of the team. People need to know and understand their co-workers' strengths and interests. How else will they know when and to whom to throw the ball? Conversely, team members feel valued when their contributions are understood by their co-workers.

2. **What is the score?** A critical managerial task is to make the organization's vision, mission, goals, and objectives come alive for the team members. Asking them to create their own measures of success will lead to commitment and not just compliance. Team members are able to judge their own work against jointly created, measurable standards, and focus their energy on the most important things that will win the "game." Making measurements clearly visible to team members, much like a game scoreboard, will keep goals on the forefront of everyone's mind.

> *"People will exceed targets they set themselves."*
>
> ~Gordon Dryden, New Zealand author

3. **How do I play?** Team members will need to know the rules, policies, procedures, and standards to play the "game." What do you do

when you buy a new board game? You probably open the box and read the directions. Maybe you play a few practice rounds before actually starting the game to make sure you understand all the steps, referring back to the directions for clarification. Team members also need training, practice, and coaching to build a culture of continuous improvement.

Let's go back to our road trip example. Your travel goal of arriving by Friday was based on your opinion on where you wanted to stop, how often you stopped, and your knowledge of your chosen route. But how does that change if there are other passengers with you on the road trip? The other passengers will have ideas on how often they want to stop or have places of interest they want to see along the way. They may also have additional information to contribute on highway conditions and areas based on their experience.

It's the same with setting business goals. Your team members may see barriers to achieving the goals from their points of view and have experience and knowledge that you don't have. Getting their input on how realistic the goals are and what barriers would have to be overcome is an important step. This also encourages commitment in achieving the goals.

One method of getting participation is to hold a goal-setting meeting with your team members. Begin by explaining the corporate goals for the year and how you see your department making a contribution. Then share your goals and ask questions to encourage participation. Here are some sample questions to consider:

1. What additional information would you like to have about our goals?

2. What barriers do you see in our achieving these goals?

3. What suggestions do you have for overcoming the barriers?

4. What recommendations do you have for adjusting our goals up or down?

5. Are there any other goals we should consider creating for this year?

6. How would these goals contribute to the organization?

In addition to participating in overall department goals, it is important for individuals to have their own goals. By setting goals, team members:

- Improve their performance

- Increase their motivation to achieve

- Increase pride and satisfaction in their performance

- Improve self-confidence

Teaching your team members the goal-setting process including the goal, resources, plan, milestones, and measurements will assist them in creating goals that are achievable and that will lead to their satisfaction and increased productivity for your overall department.

In addition to goals, your team members also need to know what other behavior expectations you and your organization have for them.

Expectations for Your Team Members

Why take the time to explain expectations to your team? After all, everyone knows what is expected... it's common sense. But what is common sense? It assumes that everyone has had the same experience, which then becomes "common" to all. When we make the assumption that we've all shared exactly the same past experience, we might neglect to keep an open mind that others are different with diverse experiences.

For example, in the USA we experience the game of football at an early age. Ask people from the UK, however, about football and they will think you are speaking about what Americans call soccer.

One of the worst things a manager can hear from a team member is, "I didn't know" or "no one told me." You may have thought that it was one of those "common sense" things and not have considered talking about it to your team members. It's better to err on the side of too much information than not enough and set your employees up for success rather than failure due to insufficient information.

Our competitive economy demands that organizations be highly productive, which in turn requires employees to meet high expectations. How effectively do you communicate your high expectations? Not communicating expectations can be compared to not explaining the rules of the game... how would anyone know how to win? When employees don't know the "rules of the game" it leads to frustration, rework, conflict, and loss of productivity.

Explaining the Rules of the Game: Communicating Expectations to New Team Members

Explaining the rules of the game is important for new employees, but it doesn't hurt to review some of the information for transferred employees as well. Remember the expectations meeting with your manager we discussed in Chapter two? You can also have an expectations meeting with your team members, utilizing several of the methods and tools described below. You have already collected many of these items for your management guidebook, discussed in Chapter Two, "Navigating Company Expectations."

- **New employee orientation**: Most companies get new employees off to a great start with an interactive orientation session that includes your company's culture, mission, and history. Typically, the human resources department manages the orientation. If it has been a while since you've attended an orientation session, it is a good idea to add your name to the schedule and hear what your new team members are being told. You can then reinforce the information or add specifics for your department after the formal orientation.

- **Handbooks/policies**: Handbooks and policies were mentioned in Chapter Two, "Navigating Company Expectations." Your team members need this information too, and most likely received these tools during orientation. You may wish to pick a few key policies to discuss with new employees to demonstrate that you consider them important and how you will be referring to the information.

- **Department operating procedures**: Expectations for specific departments can be communicated through step-by-step operating procedures if uniformity of the process is required. Examples of operating procedures are safety plans and paperwork processing steps. While policies apply globally across the company, procedure expectations are for your specific department.

- **Job descriptions**: Job descriptions are expectations that relate directly to what a person does on a day-to-day basis. Discussion of the job description can be the basis of a two-way dialog between you and your employee on what performance is expected. You can compare a blank performance review form with the job description to demonstrate how performance will be measured at the end of the review period. If your form has specific behavioral expectations, you can have a discussion using examples for each of your performance categories. Again, team members appreciate knowing how to "win the game."

- **Ground rules**: Do your employees work in groups or teams? Why not let them create their own expectations on how they intend to work together effectively. Ground rules can be created in a team meeting during a brainstorming session. Sample ground rules include only one person speaks at a time during meetings, respect personal workspace, being on time, etc. Having these ground rules come directly from your team members creates a high level of commitment.

Summary

Setting department and personal goals involves five items: the goal, resources, a plan, milestones, and measurements. Involving your team members in goal setting increases commitment and the likelihood goals will be achieved. Effectively communicating your expectations means there are no surprises and employees receive the satisfaction of feeling they are "winning the game."

Building Your Map
Follow-up Activities

1) Review or create goals for your department and your personal development. Check for the following items:

☐ Goal

☐ Resources

☐ Plan

☐ Milestones

☐ Measurement

2) Meet with your manager to verify department and personal goals from activity 1.

3) Meet with your team members to discuss department goals. Check which items you will discuss; add your own items:

☐ What additional information would you like to have about our goals?

☐ What barriers do you see in our achieving these goals?

☐ What suggestions do you have for overcoming the barriers?

☐ What recommendations do you have for adjusting our goals up or down?

☐ Are there any other goals we should consider creating for this year?

☐ How would these goals contribute to the organization?

☐ _____
☐ _____

4) Have an expectations meeting with your team members. Check which items you will discuss; add your own items:

☐ New employee orientation materials

☐ Handbook/policies manuals

☐ Department operating procedures

☐ Job descriptions

☐ Ground rules

☐ _____

☐ _____

Where to Go From Here
Helpful Training Topics

☐ Goal setting

☐ Planning

☐ Facilitation

☐ Communication

SIX

OPENING COMMUNICATION CHANNELS

Chapter Learning Points:
- Target communication to fit the needs of your audience
- Effectively utilize the communication method that best fits the situation

> *"The problem with communication ... is the illusion that it has been accomplished."*
>
> ~George Bernard Shaw, Irish playwright and Nobel Prize winner

Where Is Everyone?

You have determined the best route on your management map; you have communicated it to your team and are feeling great about starting your journey. As you travel down the road toward the accomplishment of your goals, you take a glance behind you and find out no one is following you.

Oh, no! Where are your team members? You told them when you were leaving, what roads to take, how long it should take to get there, etc., but something happened and they're not with you. Communication seems like such a simple thing. You deliver a message to someone and you're done, right? Not always. There are a number of barriers that might create interference in getting your message across.

Barriers that may be roadblocks to communication include:

- Your message isn't targeted to the audience's preferred style.

- You have used words or jargon that people don't understand.

- You picked the wrong communication method for the type of message.

- You don't have the complete attention of your audience.

Give It to Them the Way They Want It

You probably have a preference for how you like information to be presented. You may like to hear just the "bottom line" and don't want to be "bored with the details." Or maybe you get frustrated when there isn't enough detail in a communication, thinking, "How am I supposed to respond when I don't have enough information?"

Maybe you are an e-mail kind of person, "Don't interrupt me with verbal chit-chat, and just send me the information." Or perhaps you are of the opinion that real communication only happens if it's in the form of a face-to-face discussion.

You know your preferences and since you conducted a getting-to-know-you meeting with all your team members, you know their preferred styles of communication, too. Now is the time to put that insight to good use.

Communication starts with empathy. When you have empathy you are able to identify with and understand another's situation, feelings, and motives. Put yourself in your audience's shoes and ask yourself:

1. What do they *want* to know?

2. What do they *need* to know?

3. How do they like knowing it?

This is another example of WIIFM (What's In It For Me).

Let's look at an example. You need to communicate that overtime has been eliminated for the next three months due to budgetary reasons. You could send an e-mail with these simple words: "No overtime is allowed for the next three months due to budgetary reasons." Quick and easy, everyone gets the same message, cross this one off your to-do list and move on. Or did you just do an equivalent of dropping a bomb and walking away?

Consider Sara. Sara has been working at least four to six hours of overtime for the last six months. The extra money has become part of how she budgets her expenses. She reads the e-mail and thinks "How will I pay my bills?"

Mike has just been assigned a large project in addition to his regular work. He was very excited because the project would give him an opportunity to show his skills and abilities, which may lead to getting the promotion he wants. Mike reads the e-mail and thinks "How will I be able to complete all my work and do a good job on this project if I can't work extra hours?" He wonders if he should turn down the project if he can't deliver good results, putting off his desire for the promotion.

How does Linda interpret the e-mail? Linda just joined the company after being laid off three times in the last three years. It seems that every company she joins ends up having financial difficulties, which result in reduction of workforce. She focuses on the part of the e-mail that says "due to budgetary reasons" and immediately begins to worry that a layoff is again in her future. She spends the rest of the day updating her resume.

Then there is Carl. Carl never wants to work overtime due to his responsibilities in caring for his small children when he gets home. "My manager knows I can't work overtime. Why did he include me in this message?" Carl wonders.

Each of these employees will have questions and concerns and probably feel that their needs were not considered in making the decision or how it was communicated.

Would a meeting have been better? Maybe. It definitely would have allowed for two-way dialog, although some folks may not have wanted to discuss personal issues in front of the group. Would one-on-one discussions have been better? The danger here is that after you told the first person, the news would pass like wildfire before you had a chance to tell everyone. One-on-one communication also takes longer.

So in this situation an e-mail was probably the best option. Could it have been worded a little better? Perhaps adding the sentence, "I know this news impacts each of you in different ways, so I'll be following up with you individually to answer questions" accomplishes the need to get the same information out to everyone but also adds a personal touch, targeted to the individual needs of everyone.

You may not be able to always accommodate everyone's preferences for receiving information, especially if you need to communicate the same information to all your team members. You can begin by using empathy for your team members' needs and making accommodations when you can. Most people will understand that another factor to consider is that the communication method must fit the situation.

There are many communication choices available, including:

- Meetings, either in person or conference calls
- One-on-one discussions
- E-mail

- Instant messaging

The following provides information on when and which communication method is most appropriate and tips on using each method effectively.

Meeting of the Minds

Managers and meetings are a love/hate relationship. Meetings are a great way to get everyone on the same page and create teamwork by having everyone share ideas. On the other hand, they can feel like a waste of time where nothing gets accomplished.

Whether you energize your team or drain them will be based on your meeting management skills. Anyone can be an effective meeting manager with a few simple techniques.

Can you imagine creating a movie without a script? The actors wouldn't know what their roles were or what lines to say. The director wouldn't know what scenes to film or in what order. Chaos, right? Yet some folks still have meetings without agendas, so the attendees are confused about what role they should play and topics are discussed all at once without thought to priority or order.

The first order of meeting business, therefore, is an agenda. If you attend a spontaneous meeting, the first agenda item can be to create the agenda. Not just any agenda, but an agenda that respects everyone's time.

Distributing the agenda prior to the meeting will allow people to bring useful reference information.

Your company may have a specific meeting agenda template, but if they don't have one, here are a few items that can be considered for inclusion:

- Topic and the length of time allocated, organized by the most important topic first.

- Name of the presenter who will lead the discussion on the topic.

- The outcomes of the agenda item; i.e., collect ideas, make a decision, solve the problem, learn a new process, etc. In other words, why is the topic included on the agenda?

- A place to list everyone's to-do's during the meeting to encourage people to be accountable for actions after the meeting. Follow-up items, person responsible, and due date are included in this section.

Who should you invite to your meeting? The people who need to be there and can make a contribution. How many people should be at the meeting? This will be determined by what you want to accomplish. If the number of attendees is too large, not everyone will be able to participate and the meeting may go too long.

Just like in the previous referenced movie example, where the actors needed a script to know their roles; the attendees at your meeting should know their roles. You may wish to consider adding roles to your meetings. Typical meeting roles include:

- **Facilitator**: Keeps the discussion flowing based on the agenda, encourages everyone's participation, and resolves conflict.

- **Timekeeper**: Monitors the time allotted for the meeting and each agenda item. Notifies presenters when their time is about to end and the whole group when the meeting is coming to a close.

- **Note Taker**: Takes legible notes for everyone to see. May also be required to type up notes and distribute them to attendees.

- **Presenter**: A content expert who delivers information or leads a discussion as part of the agenda.

- **Coordinator**: Arranges for the meeting location logistics, equipment needed, handouts, refreshments, etc.

- **Attendees**: Focus their attention on the agenda and willingly make contributions.

The person facilitating the meeting needs to focus on keeping the meeting flowing, so someone else should volunteer to take notes. A great place to record notes is a flip chart. The advantage is that everyone at the meeting can see the notes, so nothing is hidden and people can correct any misconceptions before the end of the meeting. It is a great idea for someone to make a list of outcomes of the meetings and everything that still requires follow-up and then disseminate it to all meeting attendees.

Technology allows us to have other meetings in addition to the traditional face-to-face meetings. Conference calls or online meetings are considered virtual meetings and are a great alternative if meeting attendees are geographically dispersed. Attendees communicate in real time but usually don't see each other. Keeping everyone focused, since they are not interacting face-to-face, can be a challenge. Using agendas and meeting roles with these types of meetings can keep members engaged. Interaction is important to help minimize multitasking.

One-on-One Discussions

When should you have a one-on-one discussion? When the topic only involves that person and when it is important to have a give and take dialog on a topic.

It is a little easier to target your communication style to fit your audience when it is only one person. You can adjust your content, how you organize it, and even the speed of your communication based on what you know about your team member.

Listening skills during a one-on-one discussion are just as important as speaking. Listening is challenging. It is estimated that people screen out or misunderstand the intended meaning or purpose of what they hear in over 70% of all communications!

> *"Listening is a magnetic and strange thing, a creative force. The friends who listen to us are the ones we move toward. When we are listened to, it creates us, makes us unfold and expand."*
>
> ~Karl Menninger, author and psychiatrist

Here are a few tips to improve **listening quality**:

- **Avoid distractions**: Reduce or eliminate sound and sight distractions. Don't look at papers or e-mails during a conversation. Turn your phone, PDA, and e-mail off or on silent so you don't continue to look over when you hear a ring or beep.

- **Take notes**: Note taking keeps you focused on what is being said, in addition to creating a reference tool for later use.

- **Reflect and restate**: Before you provide your input or opinion, check to make sure you understood the message. Repeat back what you just heard to allow the other person to clarify missed or misunderstood points. Avoid interrupting the other person.

- **Show interest**: Your body language, eye contact, and facial expressions show interest in another person. Use encouraging words and sounds such as "ah-hah," "I see," "tell me more," "interesting point," etc.

- **Ask questions**: Use probing skills to learn as much as you can about the other person's point of view. Clarify who, what, when, where, how, and why, but don't let the other person feel like he or she is being interrogated!

One-on-one discussion is an important communication method for managers to master. It includes facial expressions, body language, and voice tone, all of which contribute greatly to the meaning of a message. It provides you with uninterrupted time with your team members to develop a strong working relationship.

To E-mail, or Not to E-mail: That Is the Question

What did we do before e-mail? We're all so used to e-mail that if something goes wrong and our system isn't available we get nervous and irritable and probably take it out on our IT friends.

E-mail can also create problems in communication, including:

- You can never be certain that the information was received and understood.

- It doesn't include voice tone and facial expression, it may distort the meaning of your message.

- It does not encourage the sharing of ideas in a real-time two-way dialog.

E-mail is a great tool for several reasons:

- You can give information to a large number of people at once.

- Everyone will receive the exact same information.

- It's quick and easy to use.

- People can access it when it's convenient for them, even in different time zones.

- It provides documented proof that communication was sent.

Since e-mail is a terrific tool, it's important to apply basic e-mail etiquette. What managers write is a direct reflection not only on their own professionalism, but how they represent their organization. Whether you are communicating to someone internal or to an external customer, your professional impression is impacted by not only what you say, but how you say it. It is also up to you to be a role model for the way the rest of your team communicates.

Here are a few simple e-mail ideas to implement:

Learn and utilize all the tools available on e-mail. You can set your e-mail to automatically check spelling and grammar, but that is only step one. Since e-mail only checks whether the words are spelled correctly, not if the wrong word or poor grammar is used, developing good proofreading skills is important. If proofreading is not your strength, find someone who is and ask him to proofread important e-mails before hitting the Send button.

Copy only the people who are impacted by the e-mail. Can anyone today say that they get too few e-mails? If you copy people not directly impacted by the e-mail, they may be annoyed that you gave them one more e-mail that they didn't need to open that day and may be confused about what they were supposed to do with the information. The next time you really need something from them and send an e-mail, they may just ignore it, thinking, "Oh they probably are just copying me on something" and hit the Delete key.

Use the KISS principle. One definition of KISS is "Keep it Short and Simple," which is a good thing to remember for e-mails. If e-mails are longer than what can be seen on the screen and require scrolling down to read the whole message, you have increased the chance someone will close the e-mail thinking, "I'll read this later when I have more time." Well, what happens later? E-mail after e-mail is received throughout the day and your important e-mail is now behind 100 others. What should you do if you have to communicate a large amount of information? Either put the critical information, such as the due date and importance, in the first sentence or two, with further detail below, or attach a document that can be printed or electronically filed for later reference.

> *"The newest computer can merely compound, at speed, the oldest problem in the relations between human beings, and in the end the communicator will be confronted with the old problem, of what to say and how to say it."*
>
> ~Edward R. Murrow, journalist / TV newscaster

E-mail is a form of written communication and probably has almost superseded letter writing in some companies. Using your dictionary, grammar book, and thesaurus as you write will assist you in creating professional communication that you will be proud of and that will represent who you are and your company. Remember: e-mails last forever.

Instant Messaging

In our fast-paced world, when even the speed of e-mail sometimes isn't enough, some organizations utilize instant messaging. In addition to speed and real-time communication, is the advantage of having multiple people involved in the discussion, which is especially helpful for remote locations. With instant messaging you can easily verify who is available to assist you in solving your current situation. Communication can effortlessly take place by using on-site computers or remote PDAs (personal digital assistants).

With all the benefits of instant messaging, it is also important to understand some of the challenges. As with e-mail, it does not include facial expressions or voice tone, so the intent of the message is sometimes misunderstood. Since this is fast-paced communication, it lends itself to short sentences and abbreviations. Team members also may get into the habit of using these types of abbreviations and begin using them with customers, impacting professionalism.

Text messaging can also be used in business. It's quick, instant, and also uses abbreviations. The difference between text messaging and instant messaging is that a text message will not necessarily be read the moment that it is sent. Text messaging also lacks the multiple conversation aspect of instant messaging.

At movies there usually are two reminders, if not more, to turn off or silence cell phones and avoid texting because the light from the screen intrudes on the view of others in the audience. Just as people need to be reminded to turn off distractions and enjoy the show as well as consider other's enjoyment, as a manager when you monitor communications in your department your job is to consider its effectiveness and impact on everyone.

Summary

Opening communication channels means picking the right method to fit the audience and situation. Using empathy will allow you to consider the needs of your audience. Each communication method has its pros and cons; the key is developing proficiency in each to improve understanding and productivity in your department.

Building Your Map
Follow-up Activities

1) Review the preferred communication methods of your team members.

2) Determine if your organization has a standard for establishing meeting agendas. If they don't have an agenda template, consider establishing a form or procedure. Check which items you will utilize; add your own items:

☐ Topic with the length of time allocated organized by the most important topic first

☐ Name of the presenter who will lead the discussion on the topic

☐ The desired outcomes of the agenda item

☐ A place to list everyone's follow-up to-do's

☐ _____

☐ _____

☐ _____

3) Determine if your organization utilizes roles during meetings. If they don't, check which roles you will utilize; add your own roles:

☐ Facilitator

☐ Timekeeper

☐ Note taker

☐ Presenter

☐ Coordinator

☐ Attendees

☐ _____
☐ _____
☐ _____

4) If you don't already understand all the technical tools available to you for e-mail, instant messaging, text messaging, etc., set a date to educate yourself and your team members.

5) Include an agenda item at a future meeting to talk about business etiquette in communication with your team members.

Where to Go From Here
Helpful Training Topics

☐ Listening skills
☐ Communication skills
☐ Meeting management
☐ Facilitation skills

SEVEN

GUIDING THE JOURNEY

Chapter Learning Points:
- Create a positive work climate
- Develop a coaching mindset

> *"The goal of coaching is the goal of good management: to make the most of an organization's valuable resources."*
>
> *~ Harvard Business Review*

Whether your travels take you over land, sea, or air, someone is guiding the journey.

Think about the responsibilities of a ship's captain. In addition to supervising the crew, he or she has to navigate, set and correct the course and speed, avoid hazards, ensure safety, and fulfill the mission, while providing the best overall experience for the crew and passengers. Sound familiar? Could this description also apply to managers?

As a manager, you know the mission of the organization and how your department contributes. You have the knowledge and experience to set the course for your team members as well as provide course corrections. The manager is the best person to create a positive workplace climate for employees (your crew), which leads to satisfaction for customers (your passengers).

Creating a Positive Work Climate

If you were to measure the climate of a geographical area, you might include average temperature, amount of rain, days of sunshine, days above freezing, and other weather extremes. Climate is important to a ship's captain because it influences how he navigates the ship. Work climate is the "weather" of the workplace and great managers know that work climate influences employee behavior. The work climate measurements are slightly different and include retention, productivity, innovation, and teamwork.

Just like weather climate impacts the quality of lives in an area, work climate impacts the quality of work life. A positive work climate leads to employee motivation, performance, retention, and engagement.

Think about a time when you felt engaged at work. What did it feel like? What did you accomplish? Did you feel energized, with the ability to see through problems to develop innovative solutions? Did you feel you could accomplish miraculous results and exceed all your goals? What if you could create a work climate where all your employees felt engaged? What would that do for your overall business results?

> *"Work is either fun or drudgery. It depends on your attitude. I like fun."*
>
> ~Colleen C. Barrett, President, Southwest Airlines

Managers are the key ingredient in creating the type of work climate where people feel energized and enjoy their work. Many of the concepts we've discussed so far contribute to creating a positive work climate, including:

- **Positive work relationship from Chapter Three, "Getting to Know Your Traveling Companions":** People want to be accepted for who they are and be seen as individuals, and not just a "pair of hands." Getting to know your team members' likes and dislikes will aid you in developing a work climate where team members can thrive.

- **Open communication from Chapter Six: "Opening Communication Channels":** Utilizing a variety of communication methods keeps everyone informed so your team members feel connected with each other and the company. You never want to hear "No one ever tells me anything around here." People will feel positive if their communication preferences are considered.

- **Goals and expectations from Chapter Five, "Setting Your Course and Speed":** When people know what is expected of them and what role they play to contribute to the team effort, it gives them a sense of accomplishment and involvement. People can see they are valuable members of the team.

In addition, here a few more elements that are typically present in a positive work climate:

- **Fair and consistent administration of policies:** Team members need to know that their manager complies with the policies and does not exhibit favoritism through inconsistent administration of policies. This is one way to build trust.

- **Trust among team members:** Team members who trust each other and their manager are willing to share information, help each other succeed, and don't avoid healthy conflict. They feel free to discuss concerns and ideas, knowing they will be respected for their opinions.

- **Benefit of the Doubt Approach:** When there is trust present and something goes wrong, each person is given the benefit of the doubt and not accused of wrongdoing. Listening with an open mind and with the idea that there *"must be a logical explanation"* rather than being accusatory is important.

How many of these elements are present on your team? Rather relying on just perception, you can collect facts by conducting an assessment. Your organization may already conduct a climate survey, in which case you can ask for the results for your department. If not, you can work with your manager or human resources department to request assistance in conducting a survey.

Once you have the results of the survey you can hold a brainstorming session with your team to develop a plan of action. It is best to focus on one item at a time and consider asking the following questions:

1. What is currently present on our team for this item on the survey?

2. What do you see during the work day that demonstrates this item?

3. What is missing on our team in this area? What do you see during the work day that does not demonstrate this item?

4. What should we continue doing in this area?

5. What should we start doing to improve in this area?

6. How will we know our plans have succeeded?

Establishing a positive work climate, however, is merely the first step. A work climate is not static but ever changing with new people joining the team, new tasks being added, or other changes. Just like driving down the road, you can't just point your vehicle in the right direction and never steer. There are curves in the road, traffic lights, turns to make, slow moving traffic, etc. As a manager, you will be making many course corrections with your team members.

Making Course Corrections: The Coaching Mindset

Coaching is the essential skill that managers use when making course corrections. The following situations describe team members who have strengths, but also challenges. Think about what type of course correction you might make in each situation.

Situation 1: Patti is a customer service representative. She is technically proficient in her knowledge of procedures and systems. You have observed Patti raising her voice when speaking to customers who appear to frustrate her. Not only have customers complained, but her raised voice appears to disturb others in her area who can't hear their own phone calls.

Situation 2: Michele is an accounts clerk. She is a great asset to the team; always cheerful and willing to help others. The spreadsheets she completes are not always accurate and require several revisions before they meet standards. Michele has also made errors in her other tasks.

Situation 3: Stu is a sales representative. He is great at multi-tasking, closes deals, and uses excellent interpersonal skills with clients and team members. He is required as part of his job to complete status reports. Unfortunately, either the reports don't get done without a reminder from you or are turned in about a week late.

Your belief about your people and your role as a manager, have a major impact on your success as a coach. How you think and feel has a direct impact on how you behave as a manager.

Think about the following and complete these sentences:

- People are...
- Employees are...
- Managers are...

What were your thoughts? Were your thoughts "people are interesting" or "employees are invaluable to the success of our organization"? Thoughts such as "employees are a pain in the neck" or "people are too unpredictable" will negatively impact the manner in which you interact with them.

People usually don't get up in the morning and say, "I think I'll drive my manager crazy today by doing the complete opposite of what he or she wants me to do." Of course, you might find the rare exception who is motivated in the wrong direction, but typically everyone really wants to do a good job.

> *"It's a simple truth that most people prefer 'to do things right the first time.'"*
>
> ~Author unknown

The coaching mindset involves:

- **Thinking** positive thoughts about your team members.

- **Feeling** that you want the best from your team members.

- **Acting** in such a way that your team members believe that you want the best for them.

A coaching mindset is keeping the thought *"I want my employees to be the best they can be"* uppermost in your mind during regular interactions. If you believe your employees want to do a good job, you will treat minor "off-road" incidents as simply something to patiently correct.

What did you think and feel when you read the previous situations involving Patti, Michele, and Stu? This is important because what you are thinking and feeling will be reflected in the words you use and the behavior you demonstrate during the coaching session. Some managers feel they have to take a hard approach and be angry and critical to get their team member's attention. Although this approach may work in the short term, it won't gain commitment or have a lasting positive impact.

> *"You get the best effort from others not by lighting a fire beneath them,*
> *but by building a fire within."*
>
> ~Bob Nelson, author and motivational speaker

Think about the best managers you've ever had. Chances are they believed in you and also made you believe you could accomplish amazing things. What did they do to show you they believed in you? As a manager you now have the opportunity to be someone's "best" manager and create a motivational coaching climate where people know you believe in them and that they have the power within to be their best.

Look for "Coachable" Moments

How do you let people know you want them to be the best they can be? Look for coachable moments as you interact with your team members. During your interaction, look for opportunities to praise performance, celebrate successes, give training tips, or clarify priorities.

Have you noticed that you get asked more questions when you move into your team member's work area? Some employees may be unwilling to interrupt you if they have to come to your office, but being out in their work area gives them an opportunity to ask you questions about a task or project because you are right there. What would have happened if you weren't asked the question? Could the task have been completed incorrectly? Could the project have been delayed or put aside until they had found time to come find you to ask for direction?

The concept of MBWA (management by walking around) gets you out of your office or cubicle and out where the action is. Sometimes it's difficult to get away from your phone, computer, and projects, but the benefits of interacting with your team members makes it worthwhile. One way to find the time is to take the opportunity when you have to get up anyway, such as to pick up mail, go for coffee, return from a meeting, etc.

Since you are already up and out of your office, why not stop by the work areas of a few of your team members and say "hello" and ask how they are doing.

MBWA is not spying or snooping. It is being available and approachable, while seeing firsthand your employee's challenges and barriers to success. Following are a few skills of highly effective coaches. Think about how frequently you utilize these skills:

- Openly share information
- Provide frequent feedback
- Feedback provided is both positive and negative
- Demonstrate patience
- Effectively listen and clarify understanding
- Quickly assess off-track performance
- Provide recognition for accomplishments
- Available to answer questions and concerns
- Remove obstacles that interfere with team member success
- Appear approachable and not "bothered" by questions
- Provide early feedback before problems become severe

"People who are coaches will be the norm. Other people won't get promoted."

~ Jack Welch, former CEO, General Electric

These coaching skills will be invaluable when you give feedback to your team members.

Providing Feedback for Course Correction

Providing feedback is a method you can use if you want your employees to be the best they can be. Feedback is "feeding back," like holding a mirror up for reflection; sharing observations about your team member's performance or behavior on the job. We all have blind spots where we are unaware of things in our behavior that may be adversely impacting us or others. Approaching team members with the assumption they might not have been aware of the situation contributes to your efforts to display the "I want my employees to be the best they can be" philosophy.

Sometimes managers are uncomfortable about providing feedback, thinking that the team member may become defensive. Well, people do get defensive sometimes, especially if they feel embarrassed by not recognizing that something was wrong. This should not prevent you from looking for those "coachable" moments when they arise in your environment.

Here is a story to illustrate. I travel quite often in my work. When I boarded a flight recently the flight attendant at the door of the plane whispered to me, "Your zipper is open." Of course I was embarrassed, I'm not sure I even thanked her. Afterward, I started to think how much I appreciated her taking the time to tell me, because if she hadn't I might have been walking around the airport and even meeting my client with my zipper down! This was my blind spot that day. The lesson of the story is that people may be defensive or embarrassed when you first give them feedback, but they will thank you later when they realize the possibility of spending their whole career repeating the same mistake.

If you don't give your team members feedback, you are also paying the price of delay. What are you paying by delaying or avoiding feedback?

1. The situation will probably continue.

2. Behavior patterns become harder to change the longer they go on.

3. Team members are not being allowed to become the best they can be.

4. Others may become frustrated that you, as the team member's manager, haven't provided feedback.

5. When you finally give feedback, your team member will wonder why you didn't share the information right away.

In the situations presented earlier, Patti may drive away valuable clients, Michele's errors may require repeated rework and reduce productivity, and you won't be able to assess total sales activity against sales goals until Stu gives you the information you need. Until you hold a mirror up for your team members, they won't have an opportunity to be the best they can be. Can you afford this price of delay?

> *"Treat a person as he is, and he will remain as he is. Treat him as he could be, and he will become what he should be."*
>
> ~Jimmy Johnson, American football coach

A feedback discussion can be approached like a problem-solving session. Here are a few tips that will improve your feedback skills:

- **Consider your tone and body language**: Focus on thinking and feeling that you want your employees to be the best they can be and your voice tone and body language will follow.

- **Work from strengths**: For team members to feel valued, it is important that you know and value the strengths they bring to the team. Discuss how the team member can use his strengths to work on an area in need of improvement.

- **Provide specific feedback**: Speaking in generalities will just confuse your employees. Give specific feedback, including examples, to reinforce or change behavior. Stick to facts and not assumptions.

- **Explain importance**: Discuss the impact the behavior or performance is having on the company, department, and on the team member. Remember to tune into WIIFM with your team member.

- **Ask questions**: Questions will lead your team members to identifying barriers to success and developing their own solution. Using the who, what, when, how, where, and why approach helps to analyze the situation from all aspects.

- **Use a problem-solving approach**: Coaching should be a two-way conversation. It is the manager's role to point out the situation and place it on the table for discussion. It is the responsibility of both to solve the problem. What do you think will create a greater degree of commitment: a solution proposed by the manager or one developed by the team member? The solution may not be the way you would have approached the situation, but if it works it doesn't matter.

- **Follow-up**: It is important to show your team members that you continue to care that they be the best they can be. If you notice positive changes, praise and celebration is in order. If you don't see a change, just have another problem-solving discussion.

> *"I never cease to be amazed at the power of the coaching process to draw out the skills or talent that was previously hidden within an individual, and which invariably finds a way to solve a problem previously thought unsolvable."*
>
> ~-John Russell, Managing Director, Harley-Davidson Europe, Ltd.

Summary

A manager's responsibility includes creating a positive work climate and providing coaching. A positive work climate creates engagement in your team members. An engaged workforce is committed to the success of your organization. Managers use coaching to be proactive in correcting off-track performance before it becomes severe. If you want your team members *to be the best they can be*, use a coaching or problem-solving session to provide feedback.

Building Your Map
Follow-up Activities

1) Rate your work climate on the following factors on a scale of 1 = Great place to work, 2 = Pretty good place to work, 3 = Can take it or leave it, 4 = Looking for a better place to work, 5 = Please save me:

(   ) Positive work relationship with team members

(   ) Open communication channels

(   ) Goals and expectations

(   ) Trust among team members

(   ) Benefit-of-the-doubt approach

2) Develop a plan on how to improve areas from activity 1 above; share with your manager.

3) Determine if your organization has a climate survey.   Ask to see the results for your department.

4) Lead a brainstorming session with your team to improve the results of your climate survey. Choose one item at a time. Check which questions you will use; add your own questions:

☐ What is currently present on our team for this item on the survey?

☐ What do you see during the work day that demonstrates this item?

☐ What is missing on our team in this area? What do you see during the work day that does not demonstrate this item?

☐ What should we continue doing in this area?

☐ What should we start doing to improve in this area?

☐ How will we know are plans have succeeded?

☐ _____

☐ _____

☐ _____

5) Complete the following sentences and examine your thoughts and feelings:

a. People are...

_____

b. Employees are...

_____

c. Managers are...

_____

6) Consider the following coaching skills, and rate your usage on a scale of: 1 = Use consistently, 2 = Use frequently, 3 = Use most of the time, 4 = Use sometimes, 5 = Need to start using:

( ) Openly share information

( ) Provide frequent feedback

( ) Feedback I provide is both positive and negative

( ) Demonstrate patience

( ) Effectively listen and clarify understanding

( ) Quickly assess off-track performance

( ) Provide recognition for accomplishments

(   ) Available to answer questions and concerns

(   ) Remove obstacles that interfere with team
      member success

(   ) Appear approachable and not "bothered" by
      questions

(   ) Provide early feedback before problems become
severe

7) Think about one of your team members who need feedback in order to be the best they can be. Plan a coaching situation considering:

☐ **Consider your tone and body language**: How will you focus your thoughts and feelings?

☐ **Work from strengths**:   What are the team member's strengths?

☐ **Provide specific feedback**: What specifically needs improvement?

☐ **Explain importance**: Why would it be important for the team member?

☐ **Ask questions**: What questions will you ask?

☐ **Use a problem-solving approach**: How will you ask for the team member's involvement?

☐ **Follow-up**: How will you follow up?

Where to Go From Here
Helpful Training Topics

☐ Communication skills
☐ Facilitation skills
☐ Coaching skills

EIGHT

GETTING THERE ON TIME...
Time Management Tips

Chapter Learning Points:
- Spend your time on managerial activities
- Develop effective time management techniques

"Planning is bringing the future into the present so that you can do something about it now."

~Alan Lakein, author, *How to Get Control of Your Time and Your Life*

If you were traveling alone, you would be in full control of your time and your schedule. You would decide when to leave, how fast you would travel, when and if to stop for meals, etc. At the end of your travel day, you would have a sense of being in control of your day and derive satisfaction in it. Traveling alone can be compared to being an individual contributor in your organization.

As an individual contributor, you planned your time so at the end of the day you finished your "to-do" list. You may have designed a new report, finished a detailed project, wrote a technical presentation, closed a large deal, etc. You decided how to organize your day to complete your tasks and how much time to spend on each one. If you needed to come in early or stay late, or lock yourself in "do not disturb" mode, you did it. The sense of accomplishment, when you worked on something from start to finish, usually felt pretty good.

When individuals become managers, several things happen with their time and accomplishments:

- Satisfaction comes from your team members accomplishing goals and not just your own efforts.
- Your time is in demand by others needing your assistance, which results in more interruptions.
- Assignments tend to be longer, requiring project management skills.
- The number of meetings you attend will increase.

Have you successfully made the transition to managing your time as a manager or are you still holding on to old tasks and habits?

How Are You Spending Your Time?

To ensure a successful transition, it is critical to figure out how you are spending your time. The best way to do this is to create a time log by documenting what you do every hour of every day. A time log lists the time you start and end your day and every hour in between, with a space to write every activity, no matter how small. Those folks who dislike detail might be thinking, "How boring, what a waste of time." Boring, yes, this probably won't be the most exciting task of the day, but waste of time, definitely not!

Everyone who has completed a time log has had some degree of surprise as to where they spend their time. Typical insights include:

- The percentage of time they spend on managerial tasks is lower than they thought.

- They have held on to quite a few individual contributor tasks.

- Interruptions are impacting their creativity and productivity.

- They spend a considerable amount of their day in meetings.

- They spend time completing routine reports instead of important items for that day.

Which of these insights do you expect to find when reviewing your time log? Completing a time log over several days will allow you to spot trends. The insights you receive and the trends you identify will help you improve your time management skills.

What Do Managers Do, Anyway?

You may be thinking, "How should I be spending my time? What does a manager do all day?" Here is a sample list of managerial tasks:

- Give instructions
- Train/develop
- Coach
- Plan
- Create procedures

- Set goals
- Discuss policies
- Delegate
- Review performance
- Recognize

- Give feedback
- Lead meetings
- Monitor work
- Resolve complaints
- Manage conflict

- Problem solve
- Manage projects
- Discipline
- Interview
- Manage budgets

Compare this list to your time log. What percentage of time are you spending on managerial items and how much on individual contributor activities? What is the right percentage of time for your job?

> *"Besides the noble art of getting things done, there is the noble art of leaving things undone. The wisdom of life consists in the elimination of nonessentials."*
>
> ~ Lin Yutang, Chinese writer and inventor

The best way to answer the last question is to ask your manager. Some managerial positions require that you be more hands-on than others.

I Keep Holding On

The most highly-skilled people in the department are quite often promoted to managers. The best accountant becomes the accounting manager, the best sales representative is promoted to sales manager, and the best engineer moves to engineering manager. Of course, since you are the best, you are going to be better and faster than anyone on your team. Unfortunately, what this may lead to is "holding on" to work that you did before.

An additional challenge is that you may really like the tasks you did before. You received praise and a sense of accomplishment possibly for several years. Why would you give this up? This lure may lead you to continue several tasks that maybe someone else should now be doing. Rationalization may kick in. See if some of these thoughts sound familiar:

- By the time I tell them how to do it, I can do it myself.

- Everyone is already very busy.

- No one can do it as fast or accurately as I can.

- It won't take me that long; I can still fit this task in my schedule.

All these statements have an element of truth, which is why managers universally fall into these beliefs. But they are also short-term thoughts. While you are holding on to old tasks, managerial activities are not getting done and your team members are not being given the opportunity to learn something new and develop the skills that will make them faster and more accurate.

Consider Ben. Ben has recently been promoted to client services director where he leads six client service managers who are individual contributors, a position he held prior to his promotion. Ben had an excellent relationship with his clients and has been reluctant to reassign them to the others on his team. He thinks, "I can't afford to jeopardize these deals after all the years I've worked to develop the trust my clients have in me. Also, everyone else is busy and might not have quality time to devote to my clients." In the meantime...

Danielle, the newest member of his team, is struggling with several paperwork issues and two client situations. Danielle sighs and says, "Ben never seems to have the time to coach me or answer questions. He spends so much time either on the phone with or visiting his old clients there is no time left for other things."

George, having spent two years in his position, is ready to learn how to renegotiate contracts. The person who held the position prior to Ben promised George he would receive the training this year. Ben just told him it would be easier if he handled it himself. George is frustrated because he feels he has the relationship with the client and is ready to learn the next step.

Erica, the most senior member of the team, was told she would take on most of Ben's old accounts, as well as act as backup at meetings to gain exposure for the next opportunity. She doesn't have enough to do because Ben still has most of his accounts, and she hasn't had the exposure she was promised. Erica is a high achiever and is frustrated enough to start looking for positions outside of the company.

Cindy, Ben's manager, is starting to think she has made a mistake in promoting him. She can tell that Ben is working very hard, long hours, including weekends, but he isn't getting his projects done on time. Morale seems to be down and lately, his team is bypassing him and coming directly to Cindy with questions.

Ben's reluctance to let go and manage his time differently is negatively impacting his team, his boss, and himself. So where should he start? The time log will help, along with a frank discussion with John on priorities. He can then move on to the "ATES."

The ATES: Delegate, Automate, Eliminate

Let's start with delegation. Delegation has become an essential skill for all managers. Used effectively, it provides real benefits including building employee confidence, increasing productivity, as well as freeing time for strategic managerial issues.

> *"Delegating means letting others become the experts and hence the best."*
>
> ~ Timothy Firnstahl, restaurateur and author

The delegation process begins with asking yourself the tough question: "What am I currently doing that someone else should be doing or could be doing if I trained them?" It's a tough question because the answer may be the task you enjoy the most. But letting go may be the only way to allow others to become the best.

Once you have identified the tasks, you need to determine who would be likely candidates to start performing the tasks. You can refer back to what your team members identified as future goals and training desired during the getting-to-know-you meetings you held. Will delegating the tasks assist the team members to move closer to their future goals?

> *"The effective person never asks HOW will I get to do this but rather WHO will I get to do this."*
>
> ~ Mary Cantando, author, *Woman's Advantage*

Before you approach your team member with the task to be performed, you can use your empathy to determine: "Why would he or she want to take on this task?" Some people are motivated by learning something new, others enjoy contributing to the team, and still others want career growth. The real motivator will be when the team member develops proficiency on a task and you can recognize and reward his or her accomplishments.

Ensure successful delegation by defining the outcomes in a clear and measurable way. Provide coaching for achievement of the end results, but let your employees use their creativity to make the assignment their own. A follow-up plan needs to be a balance between ensuring the task is being performed to your specifications and not wanting your employees to feel micromanaged.

After Delegate... Consider Automate

What is automation? Automation is using machines to do the work of people or making a process automatic. Usually this comes in the form of purchasing a piece of equipment or software that will save time. Or maybe you can utilize software in a better way to help you or your team members save time. For example, you could automate how data populates an Excel spreadsheet.

Good targets for automation are routine or repetitive tasks that don't require that much judgment. Ask your team members, "Have you ever thought there must be a better way?" Chances are there may be. The IT department will be a great resource for this process and working with them will give you the opportunity to use your partnering skills.

Eliminate... Getting Rid of the Unnecessary

By analyzing your time log you may find that some of the things you are doing could be eliminated or you may find that you are performing a task that someone else is also doing.

General Electric uses a program called Work-Out, which is designed to eliminate the unnecessary or duplicate work, simplify processes, and reduce bureaucracy. It involves teams of employees analyzing what they do every day and making recommendations to management on what can be eliminated.

> *"Work-Out is meant to help people stop wrestling with the boundaries, the absurdities that grow in large organizations. We're all familiar with those absurdities: too many approvals, duplication, pomposity, waste."*
>
> ~Jack Welch, former CEO of General Electric

You can use a modified process in analyzing your time log for tasks that can be eliminated. Here a few questions to get you started:

- Could several reports you produce be combined into one?

- Could a task be completed less frequently?

- Is someone else doing a similar task that could be combined with yours?

- Are there excessive steps that could be combined to speed up the task?

- What would be the consequence if you stopped doing the task?

- Who would be impacted if it was eliminated?

As you delegate, automate, and eliminate you take charge of time management. So what do you tell other new managers who marvel at your time management ability? "I ATE it!"

The Knock on the Door

You sit down at your desk to start a task and someone interrupts, saying, "Do you have a minute?" Well you know from experience that things very rarely take a minute, so how do you respond?

One way to look at the interruption is to feel bothered that you have lost your train of thought. Maybe you'll breathe a heavy sigh or appear annoyed. Another way to look at it is to see the interruption as "opportunity knocking." The opportunity may be to provide critical information or clarification to an employee who would have completed a task incorrectly otherwise. Being available can be good, especially when it helps avoid costly errors.

Another way to reframe interruptions is to remind yourself that they assist you in determining training needs. Every time you receive a question, jot it down on a piece of paper, then start to look for trends. The same questions asked over and over again identify a training need. Or perhaps you need to increase authority levels if you are required to make too many final decisions.

Questions from others may be able to be postponed. You may be able to reschedule the question or discussion for later in the day if you're facing a tight deadline by quickly finding out the urgency of the question. It is important to follow up if you have postponed the question to demonstrate that you keep your commitments and also make time for your team members.

Not Another Meeting

Does it seem like you are always in a meeting? It's not just your attendance at the meeting that takes time, but after the meeting there are usually follow-up tasks. So if you attend four one-hour meetings, half your day is gone and you've probably added about eight tasks to your to-do lists.

Let's look at Ruth. Ruth has a difficult time saying no and likes to be needed. Consequently, she frequently agrees to attend meetings back to back without a break in between. That causes her to leave early from one meeting to get to the next one on time or makes her late for her next meeting. Scheduling meetings from 9-10 a.m. and then 10-11 a.m. followed by 11 a.m.-12 p.m. doesn't give her a chance to use the restroom, never mind interacting with her team members or following up on tasks.

To save your sanity and your bladder, here are a few tips to consider:

- Practice good meeting management, as referenced in Chapter Six, "Opening Communication Channels."

- Consider delegating attendance at some meetings to your team members. It will allow them to grow by exposing them to higher level issues.

- Suggest some meetings be moved to a more convenient time or day.

- Ask if you really need to attend the meeting; will your input be critical.

- Schedule your own meetings around other regularly scheduled meetings, allowing time for other work in between.

Ongoing Tasks

After you have been in your job for a while, you will start to notice repetitive activity trends. Noticing the trends will assist you in anticipating and planning for the work ahead.

> *"It wasn't raining when Noah started the ark."*
>
> ~Author unknown

Many folks will start a project on the day it's due, even if they knew it was coming for three months. Then on the day the project is due, a crises happens in another area and you're not able to work on it until late in the day. If you miss a deadline, you will appear disorganized and probably not particularly reliable. You may try to explain by saying, "But the system crashed this morning and I had to spend the morning helping the team assisting irate customers."

Everyone understands that crises happen, but if you knew it was due for three months and didn't work on it at all before that day, you are just asking for Mr. Murphy to wreak havoc on your plan. I'm sure you're familiar with Murphy's Law: "Whatever can go wrong will go wrong, and at the worst possible time, in the worst possible way." You might as well expect a visit from Mr. Murphy and plan ahead.

Know that you need data for a monthly report? Start a folder or document and add data as you gather it throughout the month, or delegate the task of gathering data to someone on your team.

Calculate that a report is going to take 10 hours to complete? Work on it two hours a day for five days or one hour a day for 10 days to chip away at it.

Another enemy to be wary of is procrastination. When procrastination grabs us it uses its power to prevent us from achieving our goals or getting what we want out of life. It has the power to prevent timely decision making, starting or completing an important project, or making us feel less successful.

Planning ahead helps combat procrastination but you might have to take a minute to ask yourself why and when you procrastinate. Do you crave the excitement of the last-minute rush? Do you procrastinate on things that seem routine or unpleasant? Do you avoid starting something that seems overwhelming? Understanding when and why you procrastinate will help you overcome it.

"The way to get started is to quit talking and begin doing."

~Walt Disney, founder, Walt Disney Company

Project Management

Many of the tasks assigned to managers are long-term and require good project management skills. Using the planning and procrastination insights will assist with project management.

Project management starts with a completion date for your project. If you can establish your own date, you can complete an analysis of how long each step will take and then estimate a completion target. Quite often, however, a due date is given to you and in this situation you must determine when you need to start the project based on the steps required.

Your company may have project management software with tools to help in your planning. If not, a simple spreadsheet will work as you complete the following:

1. Begin by brainstorming all the tasks and subtasks required to finish the project.

2. Put the tasks in logical order.

3. Add a time-to-complete column next to each task.

4. Add columns for the resources needed to complete the tasks, including money, equipment, materials, etc.

5. Select the logical person or persons who will complete each task and add their name(s) to the worksheet.

6. Communicate the plan to the project team and ask for their input on time and resources.

7. Adjust the plan based on any new information received.

8. Obtain approval for the budget based on resources needed.

9. Monitor and report progress.

10. Celebrate success.

Becoming proficient at project management will increase your confidence, reduce stress, and ensure the stakeholders for your project are satisfied.

Summary

Managers have specific time management challenges. It is important to understand how you are spending your time and then analyze if you are spending your time wisely. Managers have several choices to assist with their time management, including delegate, automate, and eliminate. Acquiring skills to handle interruptions, meetings, procrastination, planning, and project management will assist you during your management journey.

Building Your Map
Follow-up Activities

1) Complete a time log by creating a document that lists every hour of the day with a space next to the times to record tasks and activities.

2) Analyze your time log to find:

☐ Targets to delegate, automate and/or eliminate

☐ Interruptions to identify training needs

☐ The amount of time spent in meetings

3) Determine if your company utilizes project management software.

Where to Go From Here
Helpful Training Topics

☐ Time management

☐ Project management

☐ Delegation

NINE

LICENSE TO MANAGE...
Employment Law Awareness

Chapter Learning Points:
- Understand that employment laws protect employees' rights
- Focus on simple rules for managers to avoid violating employment laws

> *"Employers have a legal duty to take appropriate corrective and preventative action the first time they learn of discriminatory conduct in the workplace. We can't stress enough the importance of employers taking adequate steps to protect the rights of all employees."*
>
> ~Mary Jo O'Neill, EEOC Regional Attorney

License to Manage

Before you can be awarded a driver's license, you typically practice driving and study traffic laws. You learn that there is a fine for speeding, driving through red traffic lights, parking near a fire hydrant, failing to stop when a school bus is stopped, and so on. You are then prepared to take your test.

Unlike a driving license, there is no management license that requires practice, study, and a test. You won't be testing your knowledge, but there are many employment laws that will be of assistance to you before venturing on your management journey.

You may have heard the expression "there ought to be a law." Laws are made to provide protection from harm and to protect rights. Employment laws are made to provide protection of rights in the workplace and protect employees from being harmed. The laws we have today are necessary to legislate the protections not afforded by companies on a voluntarily basis in the past.

The various federal employment laws read like alphabet soup: ADA, ADEA, FMLA, OSHA, COBRA, and USERRA, to name just a few. In addition to federal laws, your state has separate laws that impact your business. If your company does business globally, it may also be impacted by laws in other countries.

Obviously, labor attorneys and human resource professionals must know and understand every law impacting the workplace. Your position may not require you to know every law in depth. Managers, however, are on the "front line," interacting with team members daily. Managers are in the workplace making decisions on the spot, so it is important that they have at least a basic understanding of the rights of their employees.

Focusing on the Rights of Employees

Employment law focuses on rights in the workplace. Rather than discussing the details of each law in depth, which could fill entire volumes, let's narrow our focus to the basic rights of employees. The following are just some of the employee rights:

1. **The right to be free from discrimination**

2. **The right to a safe environment**

3. **The right to be paid for hours worked**

4. **The right to job protection**

5. **The right to file a complaint**

1. The Right to Be Free From Discrimination

Everyone should be free to come to a workplace and be judged by what they can do and not by who they are. To discriminate means to treat or make decisions based on a class or category of a person rather than individual merit.

It is illegal to discriminate in any aspect of employment, including:

- Hiring and firing
- Compensation, assignment, or classification of employees
- Transfer, promotion, layoff, or recall
- Job advertisements
- Recruitment

- Testing
- Use of company facilities
- Training and apprenticeship programs
- Fringe benefits
- Pay, retirement plans, and disability leave
- Other terms and conditions of employment

Discrimination laws were instituted because segments of our population had been excluded from job opportunities.

Harassment is a form of discrimination. Employees have a right to be free from harassment at work. Harassment is unwelcome conduct that is based on race, color, sex, religion, national origin, disability, and/or age. Harassment becomes unlawful when 1) enduring the offensive conduct becomes a condition of continued employment, or 2) the conduct is severe or pervasive enough to create a work environment that a reasonable person would consider intimidating, hostile, or abusive.

"One day our descendants will think it incredible that we paid so much attention to things like the amount of melanin in our skin or the shape of our eyes or our gender instead of the unique identities of each of us as complex human beings."

~Franklin Thomas, American businessman

---

2. The Right to a Safe Environment

Employees have a right to work in an environment that keeps them safe. The General Duty clause under the Occupational Safety and Health Act (OSHA), states that employees have a right to "a place of employment which is free from recognized hazards that are causing or are likely to cause death or serious physical harm."

Until 1970, limited laws existed to protect against workplace safety and health hazards. At that time, the number of job-related deaths and disabling accidents was staggering. Excessive workdays were lost, greatly impacting productivity for employers and wages for employees.

In 1970 employees were awarded certain rights for a safe workplace, including the following:

- Receive safety training related to their jobs

- Receive safety equipment

- Receive information on hazards and other safety issues

- Request action from the employer to correct hazards or violations

- File a complaint with OSHA if you believe that there are either violations of standards or serious workplace hazards

- Find out results of an OSHA inspection

- File a discrimination complaint

> *"For safety is not a gadget but a state of mind."*
>
> ~Eleanor Everet, safety expert

3. The Right to Be Paid for Hours Worked

Before 1938, when laws were enacted to protect employees, people were forced to work excessive hours for very little pay. Overtime laws were enacted during the Great Depression for the purpose of protecting factory workers from working unreasonable hours and encouraging businesses to hire additional employees rather than pay existing ones more. In a way, overtime is more a penalty to employers than a benefit to employees.

Employees who are in overtime eligible positions must be paid time and one-half for hours over 40 in a week. Employees cannot work "off the clock" voluntarily or involuntarily. If employees work, they must be paid. If they work overtime, they must be paid for it. It is the responsibility of the manager who knows what hours employees work to communicate the correct data for the creation of paychecks.

Your human resources department can assist you in determining which positions are overtime eligible and how to properly administer pay policies to comply with laws.

4. The Right to Job Protection

There are several federal laws that protect an employee's job if he or she needs to be absent due to military service, family or medical reasons, or performance of their civic duty. Job protection can be in the form of holding their specific job or offering a comparable job.

When an absence occurs or a team member requests time off, it is important for you to understand the request and reference your company policies and procedures. Obtain advice from your human resources professional on how to process the request and appropriately discuss the situation with your team member.

5. The Right to File a Complaint

Employees have the right to file complaints and be free from retaliation for doing so. Retaliation includes threats, intimidation, reprisals, and/or adverse actions related to employment decisions. Retaliation against an individual for filing a charge of discrimination, participating in an investigation, or opposing discriminatory practices is prohibited by law.

Here is a list of the federal agencies that will hear complaints from employees along with their stated purpose:

The Equal Employment Opportunity Commission (EEOC) is the U.S. agency created to prevent discrimination based on race, color, religion, sex, age, disability or national origin in employment and to promote programs to make equal employment opportunity a reality. www.EEOC.gov

The Department of Labor (DOL) administers a variety of federal labor laws including those that guarantee workers' rights to safe and healthful working conditions; a minimum hourly wage and overtime pay, freedom from employment discrimination, unemployment insurance, and other income support. www.DOL.gov

The Occupational Safety and Health Administration (OSHA) promotes the safety and health of America's workers by setting and enforcing standards and providing training, outreach, and education. www.OSHA.gov

The National Labor Relations Board (NLRB) governs relations between unions and employers. They enforce the statute that guarantees the right of employees to organize and to bargain collectively with their employers, and to engage in other protected concerted activity with or without a union, or to refrain from all such activity. www.NLRB.gov

Managers Are the Company in the Eyes of the Law

How you respond to employee situations is critical because you are acting on behalf of your company. Doing nothing is also a decision, which may make the situation worse. If you aren't sure how to respond, your human resources department is ready to respond with roadside assistance to avoid incurring substantial costs for your organization.

When you read the newspaper headlines, you may shake your head and think, "How did this company make such a large error that cost this staggering amount? Didn't they know they were violating the law?"

Who is responsible for making the decisions that cause these staggering costs? Was it the company making the error? What is the company? A building? No, it's the managers. Managers make decisions every day that create either success or failure for their companies. There is always a person or persons behind the decision, someone who didn't handle the situation appropriately when it presented itself.

Managers are the company in the eyes of the law. The common law concept of "vicarious liability" states that the company is liable for the negligent actions of its managers when acting in the course of their responsibilities. So somewhere within these companies is a person or persons who acted in a way that violated employment laws, and the whole company is held responsible.

Just like traffic laws, where the penalties range from a mere ticket just hurts the wallet to misdemeanors and even felonies (if the violation causes injury to a person or destruction of property) employment laws can also be extremely severe. The more you violate the laws, the more serious the situation becomes. And there is no simple equivalent to a defensive driving course for violations of employment law.

It is a full-time job to keep up with the various laws and regulations. There are landmark cases every year that change the way the laws are applied. As a manager, you probably don't have the time to invest in becoming an expert. But if you remember that employees have rights, seek advice from your human resources department, and remember a few simple basics, you will become confident in handling these types of situations.

Manager Employment Law Basics

1. **Be alert to situations that may involve employment laws.** Does the situation possibly impact the rights of your team members? If yes, consult your policies and get "roadside assistance" from human resources professionals or your legal department. Managers need to be proactive in monitoring the work area and not just wait for a complaint.

2. **Base decisions on specific business reasons.** To avoid discriminating against others always base your decisions on business reasons and not personal reasons or beliefs. When hiring, giving assignments, reviewing performance, administering discipline, etc., keep the thought *"Am I representing my company in a professional, non-discriminatory manner?"* uppermost in your mind.

3. **Do not retaliate against employees who voice complaints.** Employees have the right to register complaints. Whether or not you agree with their

complaints, team members still deserve continued professional respect.

4. **Control your emotions before speaking and acting.** We sometimes say and do things we regret when we react instead of first pausing to think. It is better to maintain a calm, professional state of mind when dealing with workplace situations.

5. **Seek advice (roadside assistance!).** Managers don't have time to be experts on employment law issues, which is why your partnership with human resources is important. Their assistance can be in the form of coaching or even role-play practice before you conduct a team member discussion.

6. **Document clearly and concisely without discriminatory words.** Check all your documents such as performance appraisals, disciplinary forms, and even e-mails to make sure you utilize appropriate language free from discrimination.

7. **Make decisions in the best interest of your organization.** As a manager, you are not just making decisions that represent yourself; you are also representing your company. Ask yourself, "How does my company want me to behave in this situation?" Remember, managers are the company in the eyes of the law.

Apply Your Knowledge

Would you know what to do in the following on-the-job situations?

1. A team member tells you that she has to take off every other week for four hours, over the next three months, to take her mother to radiation therapy. **Issues to consider:**
   a. How will you respond to the team member?
   b. Is this a "right to job protection" situation?
   c. How will the team member be paid?
   d. Is there a request form to take the time off?

2. During an employment interview, a candidate suddenly shares that she is single mom with three children and must stay home with them when they are ill. **Issues to consider:**
   a. How will you respond to the candidate?
   b. Do you consider this unsolicited information when you make your hiring decision?
   c. Is this a "right to be free from discrimination" situation?

3. You pass an employee's workstation and see a sexually explicit website on his computer. The employee sees your look of horror and says: "I'm on my lunch break." **Issues to consider:**
   a. How will you respond to the team member?
   b. What policies exist on harassment and personal use of company equipment?
   c. Is this a "right to be free from discrimination situation?"

4. An overtime eligible employee, who is very dedicated, offers to work an extra two hours to finish an important report. She says: "I know we don't have overtime in the budget, so don't worry about paying me." **Issues to consider:**
   a. How will you respond to the team member?
   b. How will you get the report completed if the team member doesn't work the extra hours?
   c. Is this a "right to be paid for hours worked" situation?

5. An employee passes you in the hallway, rubbing his elbow. When you ask him what is wrong he says he fell in the lunch room, but he's okay, no need to report it or fill out any forms. **Issues to consider:**
   a. How will you respond to the team member?
   b. What are the consequences of not reporting an on-the-job injury?
   c. Is this a "right to a safe environment" situation?

Were you comfortable in your ability to provide the appropriate response for each of these situations? To aid in responding appropriately, your company will probably have an employee handbook or policies and procedure manual that incorporates the requirements of various employment laws.

Summary

Managers face situations every day that may involve employment laws. Managers need to be aware that there are numerous employment laws that have been created to protect employee rights. Managers can represent their company in a professional way by being aware of employee rights, seeking advice from experts, and conducting their responsibilities in a professional manner.

Building Your Map
Follow-up Activities

1) Jot down how you would respond to the following situations after referring to your employee handbook/policy manual:

a. An employee tells you that she has to take off every other week for four hours to take her mother to radiation therapy.

b. During an employment interview, a candidate suddenly shares that she is single mom with three children and must stay home with them when they are ill.

c. You pass an employee's workstation and see a sexually explicit website on his computer. The employee sees your look of horror and says: "I'm on my lunch break."

d. An overtime eligible employee, who is very dedicated, offers to work an extra two hours to finish an important report. She says, "I know we don't have overtime in the budget, so don't worry about paying me."

e. An employee passes you in the hallway, rubbing his elbow. When you ask him what is wrong, he says he fell in the lunch room, but he's okay, no need to report it or fill out any forms.

2) Meet with your human resources professional or senior manager to discuss your answers to activity 1. Consider a role-play practice session.

3) Review the following websites to get a general idea of their content:

☐ www.EEOC.gov

☐ www.DOL.gov

☐ www.OSHA.gov

☐ www.NLRB.gov

Where to Go From Here
Helpful Training Topics

☐ Harassment prevention

☐ Employment law for managers

TEN

NAVIGATING ROADBLOCKS, DETOURS, AND SPEED BUMPS

Chapter Learning Points:

- Identify situations that disrupt your management journey
- Overcome obstacles with practical tips and techniques

> *"You measure the size of the accomplishment by the obstacles you had to overcome to reach your goals."*
>
> ~Booker T. Washington, American educator and author

You have carefully planned your journey and created your management map. You know how you want to go, you know when you want to go, you know your traveling companions, and you have been guiding the journey along the way. Now all of a sudden, things go wrong.

Signs appear: Road Closed! Construction Ahead! Detour! Roadblock! Slow for Speed Bumps! It's enough to make you want to throw your management map out the window. But that would be littering, plus you've put so much thought and work into your map, it is definitely worth saving.

> **"Life is what happens to you while you're busy making other plans."**
>
> ~John Lennon, English songwriter

The important thing is not to get discouraged, but see this as an opportunity to grow. Your team members will watch how you deal with adversity, so this is your time to shine as you demonstrate management skills such as flexibility, problem solving, and the ability to deal with change.

Let's look at three things you probably will encounter during your management journey:

- **Roadblocks**: Barriers that prevent you from continuing on your journey as you planned.

- **Detours**: Organizational changes that require a change in course.

- **Speed bumps**: Conflict and other team issues that disrupt the forward movement on your journey.

Roadblocks

There is actually a website dedicated to "the subject (and elimination) of roadblocks on public streets, roads, and highways," I guess that there indeed is a website for everything!

A road block is a situation or condition that prevents you from progressing toward an accomplishment. What type of situation or condition in the workplace prevents us from going forward with our plans? Here are several; you probably will think of others:

- Your budget gets cut

- You lose a key member of your team

- Technology resources are limited

- Your manager doesn't approve your plans

- You have to lay off team members

Let's take an example. Linda establishes a goal for her department to achieve 80% customer satisfaction ratings by year end. (See Chapter Five, "Setting Your Course and Speed.") She has planned to purchase outside training resources for her team members as part of the way she will achieve her plan. Jeff, her manager, calls her on Monday and says, "Linda, I've been very impressed with your goals this year. The customer satisfaction goal contributes to our overall company objectives. Unfortunately, we don't have the money in the budget for outside training resources." Understandably, Linda feels frustrated and annoyed.

> *"I can't help the way I feel right now, but I can help the way I think and act."*
>
> ~Bob Conklin, author

Her feelings of frustration and annoyance are certainly justified. How she handles her behavior from there demonstrates how she has mastered the three C's of Management: **Confidence, Competence, and Courage.** Linda has a choice, a fork in the road so to speak. The roadblock presents her with two choices. The first choice is to go down the road of resentment, complain, and avoid taking positive action. The second choice is the road to problem solving.

The road to problem solving involves these steps:

1. **Identify the current reality.** In Linda's situation the reality is that she is still expected to make the 80% goal, but it must be done without spending money.

2. **Brainstorm solutions.** Based on the new reality, you can gather people together who may have great ideas to brainstorm other solutions. In brainstorming you can set a rule that "no idea is too outlandish to consider." Sometimes it's the unusual idea that sparks a realistic one.

3. **Choose a solution.** Out of all your brainstormed ideas there will be one or two that will work the best. You can set up criteria for selecting the best solution(s) such as time, cost, resources, easy/hard, likelihood of accomplishment, etc.

4. **Create a New Plan.** You've picked a new road, so it's time to create milestones and measurements.

5. **Communicate the Plan.** All your traveling companions will need to know the new plan.

Detour Ahead

What is a detour? The American Heritage Dictionary defines it as "To go or cause to go by a roundabout way."

So that isn't too bad. You still are going to be able to achieve your objectives; you just need to adjust your time frames and the path you have to take. In the workplace, when you are presented with a detour you are dealing with change.

A detour in an organization can be in the form of reorganization, a loss or addition of a customer, new technology, changes in processes, a merger, etc. In this fast-paced world, change is inevitable, and therefore managers deal with change every day.

> *"If you're in a bad situation, don't worry it'll change. If you're in a good situation, don't worry it'll change."*
>
> ~John A. Simone Sr., author

One of the important roles of managers today is an agent of change. An effective change agent first seeks to understand the reasoning behind the change, and then helps to communicate the change to others within the organization to assist in the implementation of the change.

A good definition of change is when something old stops (the current state) and something new starts (the future state). The passage between these two states is the transition. The length of time an organization spends in the disruptive transition stage is directly linked to the effectiveness of its change agents.

Here are a few techniques that will assist you in handling the "detour" and getting your team back on the "road to success" by performing your change agent role:

- **Identify what exactly is changing and why:** A change agent finds out exactly what is changing and what is not. There may be many things that remain the same, which is equally important because it will provide your team with an "anchor" during the change. You need to understand the reasons for the change to explain it to others, so keep asking questions!

- **Plan the change:** What gets planned not only gets done, but also gets done correctly! Your change plan should include when and how you will make the change announcement, training that will be required, a timeline for implementation, and strategies to minimize the impact to productivity during the transition.

- **Communicate the change:** In absence of continuous communication, rumors have a chance to spread. Communication must be ongoing and two way with a focus on listening skills. The change agent must communicate a clear vision of the future state by describing the what, why, when, and how of the change. There is no such thing as "over communicating" during times of change.

- **Encourage involvement:** Since *"change imposed is change opposed,"* team members should be involved in implementing the change to create commitment and ownership. Ideas for involvement include encouraging action planning by team members and brainstorming ideas to remove barriers to change implementation.

- **Adapt to the needs of team members:** Everyone reacts differently to change. An effective change agent is able to adapt to each of his or her team members. During your "getting-to-know-you" meeting discussed in Chapter Three, "Getting to Know Your Traveling Companions," you may have learned how your team members prefer to deal with change. You understand their preferred style and can assist each of them while going through the change process. During change, some of your team members may want time for reflection and analysis and others will want to verbalize their thoughts and ideas immediately. This is the time for flexibility in your approach by understanding every team member's preferred interaction style.

The pace of change in organizations is not likely to slow, so you will have many opportunities to handle those "detours" as a change agent.

Hold on to Your Hat... Speed Bumps Ahead

Those speed bumps not only slow your speed, but are also pretty jarring as you go over them. Can you almost feel your head bobbing first up and then down thinking about going over one? Depending on how high the speed bump is, it may almost make you come to a complete stop.

In residential areas or parking lots, speed bumps help slow traffic and make it safer for pedestrians. Sometimes on our journey, we need to slow down too and look around to keep others safe.

But what about those speed bumps that don't serve the purpose of safety, but just jar you and prevent you from moving your department forward? A major speed bump can be conflict on your team. It's jarring for people involved in the conflict and may prevent forward movement toward your goals.

Conflict is inevitable because it is extremely unlikely that two or more people working closely together, day after day, would not disagree on something! It is almost guaranteed to create bumps along the way of your journey. Conflict can be among your team members, between you and your team members, and between you and other departments.

What do you think of when you hear the word conflict? Negative experiences or positive? Conflict can be positive because it reveals problems and encourages us to deal with them. Healthy conflict can lead to growth, innovation, and new ways of thinking. Each of us has influence and power over whether conflict becomes constructive or destructive.

> *"Conflict is inevitable, but combat is optional."*
>
> ~ Max Lucade, author and minister

Here are a few practical tips to improve conflict management (when you are in conflict) which you can pass along to your team members when they are in conflict with each other:

- **Listen first, and then respond.** Acknowledge that everyone has a right to his or her opinion but first you have to hear the other person's opinion to understand that point of view.

- **Identify the objective reason for the conflict.** Conflicts are usually related to the work environment, such as responsibility overlaps or gaps, conflicting goals and objectives, competition over scarce resources, etc. The conflict may also be related to various communication and style differences.

- **Consider all the facts.** Quite often conflict arises because not everyone has access to all the facts. Asking the questions "What do we know about the situation?" "What don't we know but need to know about the situation?" helps to get all the facts on the table for discussion and improves understanding. What you may hear is, "I didn't know that was a barrier."

- **Recognize your natural response to conflict.** Negative responses include both overpowering others and being overly accommodating to avoid conflict. Positive responses include working toward the "win-win" solution that accomplishes everyone's ultimate goal.

- **Adapt to other's style differences.** Learn the interaction preferences of your co-workers and adapt to meet their needs, such as how they like to be approached, amount of detail required, method of communication preferred, pace of the discussion, etc.

- **Work toward a future solution.** Rather than finding blame; find a solution. We can't change the past; the only thing we can change is how the situation will be resolved in the future.

"Whenever you're in conflict with someone, there is one factor that can make the difference between damaging your relationship and deepening it. That factor is attitude."

~ William James, American philosopher

Summary

During your management journey you will encounter situations that will prevent you from moving forward. When you encounter a roadblock it is time to consider your options to pick a new roadway to get you where you want to go. A detour changes the way you go on your journey. Managers, acting as change agents, successfully lead the journey in the uncharted new territory. Conflict, in the form of speed bumps, can be managed successfully by fact finding and considering everyone's point of view.

Building Your Map
Follow-up Activities

1) Think about the last change that was implemented. Review the following techniques, thinking about how the change implementation could have been improved; add other ideas:

☐ Identify what exactly is changing and why

☐ Plan the change

☐ Communicate the change

☐ Encourage involvement

☐ Adapt to the needs of team members

☐ _____

☐ _____

2) Identify and analyze a past conflict. What do you believe was the reason for the conflict? Check all that apply; add other ideas:

☐ Responsibility overlaps or gaps

☐ Conflicting goals and objectives

☐ Competition over scarce resources

☐ Communication style and preferences

☐ Behavior style differences

☐ _____

☐ _____

☐ _____

3) Determine what went well during the conflict and how it could have been improved. Check the items that may have assisted with the conflict, feel free to add your own:

☐ Listen first, and then respond

☐ Identify the objective reason for the conflict

☐ Consider all the facts

☐ Recognize your natural response to conflict

☐ Adapt to other's style differences

☐ Work toward a future solution

☐ _____

☐ _____

☐ _____

Where to Go From Here
Helpful Training Topics

☐ Problem solving

☐ Facilitation skills

☐ Managing change

☐ Conflict management

EPILOGUE

ARE WE THERE YET?

> *"Now this is not the end. It is not even the beginning of the end. But it is, perhaps, the end of the beginning."*
>
> ~Winston Churchill, former British Prime Minister

You hear the little voice coming from the back seat of the car: "Are we there yet, Mom and Dad?" Your inner voice may be also saying, "Am I there yet?" or "When will my management journey end?"

Your management journey begins with a series of "firsts," first management role, first group of team members, first staff meeting, first budget, first coaching session, first delegation, and so on. These series of "firsts" are both new and exciting, and probably present the greatest leaps you will make in your journey.

After the "firsts," every new position, team member, and project improves your skills a little more. Each gives you additional opportunities to perfect your managerial talents as you move closer and closer to your management vision. Around each bend in the road are challenges to welcome and tackle with excited anticipation.

Remember John who had his retirement party in Chapter One, "Visualizing Your Management Map." He still has not completed his management journey. John is taking his management skills and experience into his retirement years by volunteering as part of a nonprofit's board of directors. He is also looking forward to being a mentor to others by sharing what he has learned during his journey.

How will you use what you've learned on your management journey? After each experience, ask yourself:

☐ How was this experience the same or different than previous situations?

☐ What went well?

☐ What would I change the next time?

☐ How does this experience bring me closer to my management vision?

What exciting opportunities are waiting for you to experience? I hope you enjoy your journey.

"Keep learning about the world. Use your mind to the hilt. Life passes quickly and, towards the end, gathers speed like a freight train running downhill. The more you know, the more you enrich yourself and others."

~Susan Trott, author

BIBLIOGRAPHY

Albrecht, Karl and Ron Zemke. *Service America!: Doing Business in the New Economy.* Homewood, IL: Dow & Jones-Irwin, 1985.

Ayers, Keith E. *Engagement is Not Enough: You Need Pasionate Employees to Achieve Your Dream.* Charleston, SC: Elevate, 2008.

Bittel, Lester R. and John W. Newstrom. *What Every Supervisor Should Know.* New York: McGraw-Hill, 1990.

Blanchard, Kenneth and Spencer Johnson. *The One Minute Manager.* New York: Berkley Books, 1983.

Buckingham, Marcus and Curt Coffman. *First, Break All the Rules: What the World's Greatest Managers Do Differently.* New York: Simon & Schuster, 1999.

Byham, William C. and Jeff Cox. *Zapp! The Lightning of Empowerment: How to Improve Productivity, Quality and Employee Satisfaction.* New York: Ballantine, 1998.

Collins, James C. *Good to Great: Why Some Companies Make the Leap and Others Don't.* New York: Harper Business, 2001.

Conklin, Robert. *Be Whole!* Eden Prairie, MN: Clifftop Publishing, 1997.

Covey, Stephen R. *The 7 Habits of Highly Effective People:Powerful Lessons in Personal Change.* New York: Simon Free Press, 2004.

Fritz, Roger. *Think Like a Manager: Everything They Didn't Tell You When They Promoted You.* Franklin Lakes, NJ: Career Press, 2001.

Harvey, Eric & Al Lucia. *Walk the Talk.* Dallas, TX: Performance Publishing, 2003.

Lakein, Alan. *How to Get Control of Your Time and Your Life.* New York: New American Library, 1974.

Lee, Shirley Fine. *R.A! R.A! A Meeting Wizard's Approach.* Amazon.com: BookSurge Publishing, 2007.

Lencioni, Patrick. *The Five Dysfunctions of a Team: A Leadership Fable.* San Francisco, CA: Jossey-Bass, 2002.

Lencioni, Patrick. *The Three Signs of a Miserable Job: A Fable for Managers.* San Francisco, CA: Jossey-Bass, 2007.

Redd, Sharon. *Totally Alive: 7 Simple Habits to Live By.* Texas: WellSpring Press, 2005.

Straw, Julie and Alison Brown Cerier. *The 4-Dimensional Manager: DiSC Strategies for Managing Different People in the Best Ways.* San Francisco, CA: Berrett-Koehler, 2002.

Swindall, Clint. *Engaged Leadership: Building a Culture to Overcome Employee Disengagement.* Hoboken, NJ: John Wiley & Sons, Inc., 2007.

RESOURCES FOR YOUR MANAGEMENT JOURNEY

Management Skills Resource, Inc. is your resource for all your management development training needs. Our products and services are dedicated to the advancement and on-the-job application of effective management principles.

Building the *competence*, *confidence*, and *courage* of your management teams through:

Classroom Training - Using proven templates, we custom design workshops based on your company's culture, policies and procedures.

On-Line Training - Each on-line course contains interactive exercises, simulations, and assessment tools, including a pre and post test so that it's easy to measure knowledge acquisition.

Assessment Tools - Our learning instruments are always designed to align people's skills and behavior with organizational strategies.

Management Skills Resource, Inc.

www.ManagementSkillsResource.com
Info@ManagementSkillsResource

ABOUT THE AUTHOR

Deborah Avrin, MS, SPHR, brings over 20 years of human resources and training experience to her company, Management Skills Resource, Inc. Her coaching skills have assisted countless managers to improve their performance in such diverse industries as financial services, manufacturing, utilities, transportation, education, non-profit and telecommunications.

Prior to beginning her consulting practice in 1998, Deborah Avrin held a variety of top-level human resources leadership positions in both the financial services and manufacturing industries. She also has held operational management positions, which enables her to understand the unique training needs of managers. Her reputation is as a motivator, with an inspiring training style that encourages others to excel.

Her company, Management Skills Resource, Inc., works with organizations that want to build the confidence, competence and courage of their management teams through creative training workshops.

Her educational background includes a BBA in human resources and a masters degree in organizational behavior. Deborah Avrin also holds a lifetime Senior Professional in Human Resources (SPHR) certification.

www.ingramcontent.com/pod-product-compliance
Lightning Source LLC
Chambersburg PA
CBHW060608210326
41519CB00014B/3597